VIRTUAL
LEADERSHIP

The Essential Principles
for Remote Work

BART BANFIELD

Foreword by J. C. Watts

Virtual Leadership
The Essential Principles for Remote Work

Copyright © 2020 by Bart Banfield

Published by Lucid Books in Houston, TX
www.LucidBooksPublishing.com

Scripture quotations are taken from the Holy Bible, New International Version®, NIV®. Copyright © 1973, 1978, 1984, 2011 by Biblica, Inc.™ Used by permission of Zondervan. All rights reserved worldwide. www.zondervan.com The "NIV" and "New International Version" are trademarks registered in the United States Patent and Trademark Office by Biblica, Inc.™

ISBN: 978-0-9962441-5-2
eISBN: 978-1-63296-414-4

Special Sales: Most Lucid Books titles are available in special quantity discounts. Custom imprinting or excerpting can also be done to fit special needs. Contact Lucid Books at Info@LucidBooksPublishing.com.

Table of Contents

To my wife, Jennifer, who has been by my side for nearly a quarter of a century. Your continued support and belief in me have served as my foundation throughout our journey together. Your dedication to our three children and your example of selfless love inspire me. I love you.

Foreword

I first met Bart Banfield in the spring of 2002 at an athletic awards banquet put on by my alma mater, Eufaula (OK) High School. I had been asked to speak to the student-athletes and their families about the role athletics can play in teaching life lessons to young people. Bart had just finished another successful season as the head girls' basketball coach at Eufaula High School, and having grown up in the Eufaula community, I knew firsthand the passion members of that community feel about their local sports teams.

I would not reconnect with Bart until after he had accepted the superintendent's position at Stidham Public Schools. My wife and I own a ranch outside Stidham, approximately 13 miles northwest of Eufaula, and each summer we invite friends and family from around the country to an old-fashioned cookout to celebrate our country's independence. The cookout has grown exponentially since its inception, so I found myself in need of additional tables and chairs. I reached out to Bart about the possibility of borrowing tables and chairs from his school's cafeteria. When we went to pick them up, I was able to sit down and spend some time getting to know this young leader. He was hungry for knowledge and some of the wisdom I had acquired over my years as a leader in different circles, and he was like a sponge. He asked lots of questions and listened intently as I talked about topics such as faith, family, and athletics and the pivotal role they had played in my life. I have had the privilege of mentoring a few individuals throughout my lifetime and I could tell that Bart had a desire to be molded, to learn, to grow and strive to do life and leadership well. I invited Bart, his wife, Jennifer, and their children to my family cookout that summer, and they accepted.

What started off as a simple introduction has evolved into a friendship that has spanned almost two decades. Bart moved on from his superintendent's role at Stidham Public Schools, but we have stayed in contact with each other. Bart has reached out on several occasions for advice during the ups and downs of life, and I believe we have a responsibility to shepherd and share our wisdom and experiences with those who are seeking guidance. I am proud of the success Bart has achieved, and I am proud to have been able to sow into his life to assist in his leadership roles, encouraging him to become the best leader he can possibly be.

Embedded within this book are timeless principles that have served me throughout my life as a husband, father, grandfather, professional athlete, businessman, minister, and congressman. I continue to apply lessons like these each day in my life. I am confident they will serve as a solid foundation for you in your journey.

Leading with a servant's heart—the right heart—is critical as we go further into this new digital era. Technology has made our lives different today than they were 20 years ago, and it will make our lives different 20 years from now than they are today. It is constantly changing our lives both personally and professionally. *Virtual Leadership* is a glimpse into the future as we seek clarity concerning life and leadership in an ever-changing world.

—J. C. Watts Jr., served eight years in the US Congress, ordained minister, athlete

Introduction

Your life is about to change. Embedded within this book are ideas and lessons that have been passed down from one generation to the next for centuries. My only goal behind writing this book is to take the principles I have acquired, couple them with the experience and lessons I have learned in over 20 years of working in a variety of leadership positions, and merely *pay it forward*.

These leadership principles have been tested over time and have proven to be the necessary ingredients to create success. If you choose to apply them in your life, you will achieve more peace and prosperity than you ever thought possible. Your results will be contingent on the effort you put into applying these lessons.

Success comes in many colors, but make no mistake, it all comes from behind the same door. The problem for you and millions of others like you is that the door is currently locked. The door requires a key to unlock everything you want in life. Not any key will do. The key must be the right size and shape, and it must be turned in the proper sequence to unlock the door of success. Along with the key is a willingness to open your mind to the belief that if you want something bad enough and are willing to follow in the footsteps of others who have traveled this path and achieved similar results, you can have it.

I know because I have the key, and I have unlocked the door. I am no different than you. The son of a public-school educator with modest means, I was not born with a silver spoon in my mouth. I began my climb over 20 years ago and have successfully reached the summit of my profession. My goal is to help you achieve the summit too.

I have studied leadership throughout my life and have read hundreds of books, allowing me to become an authority on the topic. Most of the leadership principles in this book are not mine. This book is full of quotes and leadership principles from authors who have been influential in my life. The principles embedded within this book have come from those who walked this trail before me and have been kind enough to *pay it forward* so a small-town Oklahoma kid from humble beginnings could achieve his dreams. I am grateful to those who came before me. My goal is to gather all the leadership principles I have acquired into one book and simplify the complexity of the leadership gauntlet. I want to encourage you to pay close attention to the sequence of the leadership principles. Learning can be linear, and many of the concepts and methods build on one another.

Before we begin our journey together, I want you to know one thing. I believe in you. When you practice these principles in a disciplined fashion, you will begin to see your life change in a positive direction. Waiting at the completion of this book is the answer you desire. The blueprint of success in your life is right behind this door. Turn the page and unlock your future.

CHAPTER 1

Nature vs. Nurture

The key to success is to focus our conscious mind on things we desire not things we fear.

—Brian Tracy

re leaders born, or are they made? This debate has been ongoing for centuries. I believe nature is neutral. On one hand, genetics can certainly enhance characteristics consistent with leadership traits; however, there is no doubt that the environment in which one grows up impacts and molds the individual. The key is control or, more precisely, the locus of control.

In 1954, American psychologist Julian B. Rotter developed the concept known as locus of control, which is the degree to which people believe that they have control over the outcome of events in their lives. An individual with a strong internal locus of control believes that events in their life derive primarily from their actions. However, an individual with a strong external locus of control will tend to praise or blame external factors. If nature is neutral, where do you fall in the locus of control debate? Do you believe you are the captain of your ship and in control of your destiny? Or, do you feel you are a victim of circumstance in this complex world?

Consider this quote commonly attributed to best-selling author Brian Tracy: "Control begins with your thoughts. Your thoughts determine your feelings. And your feelings determine your actions." Control becomes the fulcrum of our emotions and the decisions that follow. If you don't like where you are in life, you can choose to change. In his book *Emotional Intelligence*, author Daniel Goleman summarized why emotions can overwhelm our thoughts:

> Evolution gave humankind emotions to help people cope with dangerous situations and to act in the face of peril. Modern people retain the emotional system of their cave-dwelling ancestors, who regularly faced life-and-death situations. In modern society, those emotions often over-whelm logical thought. In a real sense, each person has two minds, one that thinks and one that feels. The rational mind lets a person ponder and reflect. But the emotional mind is impulsive and powerful. Usually, the two work in harmony, but intense feelings sometimes allow the emotional mind to dominate the rational mind.[1]

Have you ever been so upset that you struggle to sleep at night? The feeling of being unsettled is an example of your emotional mind dominating your rational mind. The ability to control both minds requires emotional intelligence. The term *emotional intelligence* first appeared in a 1964 paper written by Michael Beldoch. Emotional intelligence refers to "the capability of individuals to recognize their own emotions and those of others."[2] Adjustment and adaptation are necessary leadership characteristics in a twenty-first-century world, which is ever changing.

---

1. Daniel Goleman, *Emotional Intelligence: Why It Can Matter More Than IQ* (New York: Bantam Books, 1995), E-book.
2. Kin Wai Michael Siu and Yi Lin Wong, *Practice and Progress in Social Design and Sustainability* (Hershey, PA: IGI Global, 2018), 235.

Author Kevin Cashman summed up leading from the inside out when he stated: "Leading others requires mastering yourself first. The essence of leadership is growing the whole person to grow the whole leader."[3] Assessments of thousands of leaders showed that those who lead from the inside out have three essential personal competencies:

1. **Authenticity** – They are self-aware and know who they are. They understand their own strengths, vulnerabilities, and development challenges.

2. **Influence** – They communicate honestly about their true values and priorities to build connections with other people.

3. **Value creation** – Through their actions, they serve their team, organization, world, family, community, and themselves with passion and aspiration.

Authenticity is the currency of twenty-first-century leadership. Leaders must be willing to demonstrate vulnerability. Organizations that are growing at a dynamic rate are always evolving to keep up with the ever-changing demands of the customers they serve. It is impossible to know the answer to every question. As I have matured as a leader, I have learned to say, "I don't know the answer to your question, but I will find out and get back to you." By making myself vulnerable, I demonstrate to those I lead that it is okay to be vulnerable too. Another wonderful way to demonstrate vulnerability is by sharing a personal story of failure, followed by the lesson you learned along the way. John C. Maxwell had this to say about failure: "The difference between average people and achieving people is their perception of and response to failure."[4] Life is a journey full of highs and lows. No one

---

3. Kevin Cashman, *Leadership from the Inside Out: Becoming a Leader for Life,* 3rd ed. ReadHowYouWant.com.
4. John C. Maxwell, *The Maxwell Daily Reader: 365 Days of Insight to Develop the Leader Within You and Influence Those Around You* (Nashville, TN: HarperCollins Leadership, 2011), 61.

is immune to the pitfalls of life, and sharing teachable moments can expedite the learning curve of those you lead and create a perception of authenticity.

Authenticity does not come easily. It comes through consistent deposits of time. Authenticity will allow you to build a bridge to influence those you lead. According to John C. Maxwell:

> True leadership cannot be awarded, appointed, or assigned. It comes only from influence, and that cannot be mandated. It must be earned. The only thing a title can buy is a little time—either to increase your level of influence with others or to undermine it.[5]

Credibility can be hard to come by, especially if you are a young and inexperienced leader.

It was May 2003, and at the tender age of 27, I became the youngest public-school superintendent in the state of Oklahoma when I took the helm at Stidham Public Schools. I was full of passion and ideas about how I was going to change the world. One of the first projects I wanted to tackle that summer was a makeover of the school building, including new carpet for every classroom. To save the district money, I decided to rip the old carpet out of each classroom. What I didn't know at the time was that the original carpet had been glued to the old wooden floor that served as its original foundation. The carpet had to be scraped, tugged, and pulled to be removed. This process took not hours—but days for our custodial staff and me to complete. Removing carpet is backbreaking work. Instead of wearing a collared shirt and tie to work as the new superintendent, I wore overalls and work boots. Day by day and classroom by classroom, we chipped away at the task at hand, and something began to change. After weeks of work, I began to be viewed

---

5. John C. Maxwell, *The 21 Irrefutable Laws of Leadership Workbook* (Nashville, TN: HarperCollins Leadership, 2007), 14.

not as an outsider but as someone who was willing to roll up my sleeves and pull my own weight. The time invested each day was an opportunity for me to get to know my new colleagues and for them to get to know me. It was there that I learned a valuable leadership lesson. Don't expect your new team members to come to you; instead go to them. When the project was complete, and the new carpet had been installed in every classroom, a minor renaissance had been achieved. Just as important, though, I had earned the respect of my new colleagues. They began to follow my lead, not because they had to, but because they wanted to.

Influence is the definition of leadership in the twenty-first century. Influence is the by-product of honest communication and the ability to create and sustain a connection with those you lead. So how do I connect with a brand-new team, you ask? By finding common ground. Take a look back into your past for common ground. In some cases, it may be a personal experience, such as where you went to school or people you know. Finding common experiences such as being parents or grandparents might be the ticket. In other cases, it may be a professional experience, such as serving in a similar role in your previous place of employment. Common ground creates a connection that, if fostered over time, builds trust with those you lead.

Trust is the foundation of leadership. Author Stephen R. Covey had this to say about trust: "Trust is the glue of life. It's the most essential ingredient in effective communication. It's the foundational principle that holds all relationships."[6] It is important to remember that trust is not given; trust is earned. The phrase "say what you mean and mean what you say" resonates with me when it comes to cultivating trust. Trust is the cause, and influence is the effect.

Influence is the secret sauce that distinguishes a mature leader from an immature leader. Author Ken Blanchard says, "The key to

---

6. Stephen R. Covey, quoted in Hilarie Owen, *Creating Leaders in the Classroom: How Teachers Can Develop a New Generation of Leaders* (United Kingdom: Taylor & Francis, 2006), 150.

successful leadership today is influence, not authority."[7] So, are you leading through authority or influence? Leadership through fear and intimidation is leading by authority. I call these types of leaders, dominators. Leadership through empowerment or liberation creates a pathway to influence. Influence is the nucleus of team building. With influence, you can begin to tap into the power of multiplication.

Two is better than one, and one is better than none. According to Rory Vaden, a global expert on self-discipline and productivity:

> Multipliers don't think about today; they think about tomorrow, and the next day, and the next day, something that we refer to as the significance calculation. How long is this going to matter? In other words, how is this going to matter tomorrow, or the next day, or the next day? The significance calculation changes everything. You multiply time by spending time on things today that give you more time tomorrow.[8]

Multiplication allows a team and, thereby, an organization to create a virtual mechanical advantage. Let's use the balance beam as an analogy: A lever amplifies an input force to provide a greater output force, which is said to provide leverage. Multiplication creates momentum, and leverage allows organizations to scale greater heights and discover maximum value creation. How high an organization will climb is in direct proportion to how deeply it is committed to a purpose.

Know What You Want and Why

Have you ever stopped and pondered what your purpose is? Or are you simply living from paycheck to paycheck trading your time for someone

---

7. Ken Blanchard, quoted in Bob Nelson, *1001 Ways to Take Initiative at Work* (New York: Workman Publishing Company, 1999), 75.
8. Rory Vaden, "How to Multiply Your Time," TED Talk, June 1, 2015, https://youtu.be/y2X7c9TUQJ8.

else's money? There is nothing you can do to create more time inside the construct of one day. We are all given the same 24 hours or 1,440 minutes or 86,400 seconds. The German theologian Albert Schweitzer believed that "the purpose of human life is to serve, and to show compassion and the will to help others."[9] What is your organization's purpose? Does your organization have a mission statement and a set of values or beliefs? Are those values congruent with how you define success?

In *See You at the Top*, American author Zig Ziglar said, "You can have everything in life you want if you will just help enough other people get what they want."[10] How would the people you lead describe you? Are you more interested in service or self? Remember, your actions speak much louder than your words. Cultivate an attitude of gratitude, and you will be amazed at what you attract into your life.

Self-improvement expert Dale Carnegie stated that "happiness doesn't depend on any external conditions; it is governed by our mental attitude."[11] Your attitude is a derivative of your expectations. Consider this quote commonly attributed to author Brian Tracy: "A positive attitude makes all the difference. Attitude is how you view things. Your self-concept controls your beliefs, which determine your expectations. This is the 'master program' of your life, the bedrock."

Expectations are set based on a standard. Have you set a standard of excellence for yourself and the people you lead? If not, I want you to know that it is hard to hit a target you cannot see. Most people will simply drift from one day to the next with little to no direction. Be intentional about your expectations and attitude. Understand that hope is always on the horizon.

---

9. Albert Schweitzer, quoted in John C. Maxwell, *The Complete 101 Collection: What Every Leader Needs to Know* (Nashville, TN: HarperCollins Leadership, 2012), 305.
10. Zig Ziglar, *See You at the Top* (Mount Pleasant, SC: Arcadia Publishing, 2010), 45.
11. Dale Carnegie, quoted in Cornelius Jones, *Inspirational Being* (2012), Lulu.com.

Developing an internal attitude of optimism will produce an external increase in performance. Consider this quote commonly attributed to Daniel Goleman:

> Psychologists have identified a peak-performance state called "flow," which musters the most positive use of emotional intelligence. Flow is the feeling you have when you are fully engaged in a task where you have advanced skills and love the work involved.

Are you and your team operating at an optimum level of performance, or flow?

There is a mental law known as the Law of Attraction. Consider this quote commonly attributed to Brian Tracy:

> You are a living magnet, and you attract into your life the people and the circumstances that are in harmony with your dominant thoughts. In the universe, all energy is in a state of vibration, including mind energy. Your mind is incredibly powerful but it is a neutral law. If you think negative thoughts you will attract negative things into your life as well.

Truly successful people expect to be successful. They enjoy the clarity that comes with confidence about the future. They enjoy a symbiotic relationship between their inner world and their outer world. Consider this statement commonly attributed to Stephen R. Covey:

> Certain basic principles and values make people more effective. They are fairness, equity, integrity, honesty, human dignity and worth, excellence, a spirit of service, patience, perseverance, nurturance, caring, courage, encouragement, and the can-do attitude that recognizes boundless potential. The person whose character grows

from these classic principles is a leader who, having mastered him or herself, can inspire and help others.

Let me ask you a question: What do you want? I would encourage you to take a minute to stop and think about the goals you want to achieve in your lifetime. Begin with the end in mind and work your way backward. What you will find is that in many cases, the stops you made along your professional journey have been stepping-stones or teachable moments that have allowed you to get where you are today. I can say from experience that growth is painful. It is like a roller coaster filled with ups and downs. The greatest lessons I have ever learned as a leader derived from some of the most painful experiences of my life. Remember, real growth occurs just outside your comfort zone.

Once you have determined what you want, ask yourself this question: Why do I want it? English Philosopher Thomas Hobbes (1588–1679) asserted that "human desire is the fundamental motivation of all human action."[12] Understanding the why creates a connection between where you are and where you want to be. The why also builds perseverance or grit during the highs and lows of your journey. Now that you know what you want and why you want it, this is the time to focus on your growth and development.

Growth and Development

Developing your skills is what separates a leader from a follower. Have you ever heard the saying, "no pain, no gain"? Developing your skills over an extended period will require one word, *discipline*. American author Jim Rohn said that "discipline is the bridge between goals and accomplishment."[13] Self-discipline requires persistence to continue

---

12. Thomas Hobbes, quoted in Bailey Forrest and Y. Lin, *Systemic Structure Behind Human Organizations: From Civilizations to Individuals.* (New York: Springer Publishing, 2011), 347.
13. Jim Rohn, quoted in Harold Wallace and A. Masters, *Personal Development for Life and Work* (Boston: Cengage Learning, 2010), 427.

developing your strengths and improving your weaknesses. Have you identified what your shortcomings as a leader are? Not sure? Ask the people you lead to fill out an anonymous survey, and you will very quickly discover what skills you need to improve. Remember, every leader has natural strengths and weaknesses. Do not neglect these areas, or they will become blind spots that hinder your ability to grow and maximize your potential.

In the spirit of transparency, I am going to share one of my weaknesses that I am still struggling to improve after 20 years of working in a leadership capacity. For me, patience is still an area that I need to strengthen. Author and speaker Joyce Meyer said: "Patience is not simply the ability to wait—it's how we behave while we're waiting."[14]

I am reminded of a time when I was working as a brick-and-mortar superintendent. It was a hot spring day during the month of May, and our students had been outside playing during their recess time. One of the highlights of coming inside from recess was the opportunity for students to purchase a vanilla soft-serve ice-cream cone for a quarter. I was sitting in my office when one of our students came into the administrative assistant's office with a look of panic on his face.

My administrative assistant asked: "What's wrong, Billy?"

Billy had turned white as a ghost, and he explained to us that he had placed the quarter that he was going to use to purchase his vanilla soft-serve ice-cream cone into his mouth.

My administrative assistant said: "And?"

Billy sheepishly replied: "And I accidentally swallowed it."

My administrative assistant said: "Well, Billy, I guess you're just going to have to be patient and wait for it to come out the other end."

Billy looked puzzled and asked: "So I am not going to be able to get my ice-cream cone today?"

My administrative assistant said: "Probably not today, Billy."

---

14. Joyce Meyer, quoted in Jennifer LeClaire, *Dream Wild: Ignite Your Faith to Defy Impossibilities* (Lake Mary, FL: Charisma House, 2018), 86.

Billy, still looking puzzled about the possible digestion of a quarter through his intestinal tract, asked a follow-up question: "Will it still come out a quarter?"

Without skipping a beat, my administrative assistant said: "Well, Billy, if it comes out two dimes and a nickel, you come back and see me."

Billy left the office bewildered that day, having learned two valuable lessons in life. One, don't put your money in your mouth, and two, patience is priceless.

We live in a global society that is always on. This 24/7 mentality has trickled into the economy and into organizations wanting to maintain a competitive edge. Both production and performance dominate the twenty-first-century workplace. It often feels like there is never enough time to meet the constant demands. Sometimes, I lose sight of the fact that the virtual or remote work environment creates complexities and challenges that the traditional work environment may not.

For example, time is a variable. When you start work and when you finish work could vary from day to day or week to week in a remote work environment. The traditional (nine-to-five) rules of the twentieth century may not apply in the twenty-first century. With the invention of smartphones, we always have a computer in our pocket to answer just one more email or text message. We are in constant contact with one another. However, twenty-first-century leaders must discipline themselves to demonstrate restraint when it comes to communication. Over my career, I have learned the hard way to be patient when it comes to contact with those I lead and with others in general.

My wife, Jennifer, is one of the most giving people I know. However, one area she refuses to give in on is quality time. She expects me to be a provider when I am at work, and she also expects me to be a husband and father when I am at home. Leading an organization of over a thousand employees can be time-consuming, and occasionally, I fail to balance my work responsibilities and my family responsibilities appropriately. Jen will quickly remind me she has been with me from the beginning of this journey, and she and our three children are my number one priority. As usual, she is right, and I am wrong. Eventually, I will recalibrate my time and priorities. Author Jim Rohn had this to say about priorities: "Either you run the day, or the day runs you."[15]

What are your blind spots? Where can you improve? What are you doing today to improve your tomorrow? Remember, what you want tomorrow, you have to do today. For some, the answer may be to go back to school. For others, the answer may be to learn a new trade or skill. Soft skills, coupled with hard skills, are also valued currency in the twenty-first-century economy. Knowledge has never been more readily available than it is today. Your success, however, hinges on desire. Napoleon Hill said that "the starting point of all achievement is desire."[16] What motivates you? Let's take a slight detour and see whether we can determine what intrinsically motivates you.

Know What Motivates You

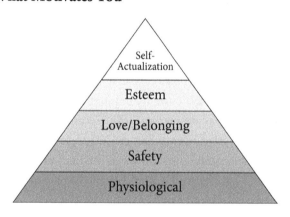

Most leaders learn about Abraham Maslow and his hierarchy of needs during their secondary or post-secondary studies. This psychological theory was first described in Maslow's 1943 paper, "A Theory of Human

---

15. Jim Rohn, quoted in *Job Readiness for Health Professionals – E-Book: Soft Skills Strategies for Success* (New York: Elsevier Health Sciences, 2016), 12.
16. Napoleon Hill, quoted in Les Taylor, *Moving from Activity to Achievement: Keys for Transforming Your Life and Your Business* (iUniverse, 2009), 4.

Motivation," and then later published as a book under the same title.[17]
Maslow's hierarchy of needs demonstrates how humans intrinsically
take part in behavioral motivation. For motivation to occur at the
next level in the pyramid, each level below must be satisfied within
the individual. Maslow's theory is fundamental to understanding how
motivation and drive are correlated in human behavior. At the top of
Maslow's hierarchy of needs is the level of self-actualization. Sometimes
referred to as transcendence or servant leadership, self-actualization
is achieved when the leader gives himself or herself away to a higher
calling—something bigger than themselves. Success, therefore, is found
in self-actualization. Consider this quote and definition of success by
John C. Maxwell:

> Before you begin your journey toward success, you must
> have a definition of what it takes to be truly successful.
> Many people have the wrong definition. They think
> that success comes in the form of money or power,
> achievements, or possessions; others think that success is
> the pursuit of happiness, though their quest for it makes
> them continually miserable. Success is not a destination;
> it is a process. Success comes from having a mission in life
> and knowing how to grow to fulfill it.[18]

Ultimately, you will reap what you sow in this life. You have a
responsibility to grow those you lead through mentoring and coaching.
Building others requires a time commitment, followed by consistent
encouragement and feedback. Are you growing those you lead? If
carefully cultivated over time, your mentoring of others will build your
influence.

---

17. Abraham Maslow, *A Theory of Human Motivation* (India: General Press, 2019).
18. John C. Maxwell, *Your Road Map for Success: You Can Get There from Here*
(Nashville, TN: Thomas Nelson Publishers, 2002), E-book.

CHAPTER 2

Influence

Leadership is not about titles, positions or flowcharts. It is about one life influencing another.

—John C. Maxwell

an I trust you? This is the fundamental question that the individuals you are leading ask themselves when they have to choose whether to follow your lead. Remember, trust is not given; trust is earned. Trust is the fabric by which influence is woven. Influence requires the people you lead to be malleable and willing to conform. Five key principles are essential for virtual leaders building influence with those they lead:

- Authenticity and Vulnerability
- Transparency and Integrity
- Character
- Learning
- Empowerment

Deciding to comply and follow the leadership of someone new is a fundamental choice that requires cooperation. American businessman Gary Hamel stated: "You can't build an adaptable organization without adaptable people—and individuals change only when they have to, or when they want to."[1]

Authenticity and Vulnerability

Before the people you lead decide what they think of your vision, they decide what they think of you. Establishing trust requires leaders to be active listeners. Did you know that most people speak about 170 words a minute, but they can listen to 400 to 500 words a minute? American minister Andy Stanley warned that "leaders who don't listen will eventually be surrounded by people who have nothing to say."[2] Active listening demonstrates warmth and a caring attitude. Active listening also demonstrates empathy and vulnerability, which are key ingredients necessary for building trust. Trust is a willingness to be vulnerable. In mathematical terms, the formula would read: empathy + vulnerability = authenticity.

When it comes to authenticity, your actions speak louder than your words. I have learned over 20 years in a variety of leadership roles that showing vulnerability is a sign of strength and courage. American author Brene Brown is an expert on the topic of vulnerability in leadership. She says that "vulnerability is the birthplace of connection and the path to the feeling of worthiness. If it doesn't feel vulnerable, the sharing is probably not constructive."[3] If you can be vulnerable with those you lead, chances are those individuals will make themselves vulnerable with you. Unfortunately, most leaders treat relationships like a transaction, asking the people they lead: "What can you do for me?"

1. Gary Hamel, *What Matters Now: How to Win in a World of Relentless Change, Ferocious Competition, and Unstoppable Innovation* (Germany: Wiley, 2012), E-book.
2. Andy Stanley, quoted in Vinnie Venturella, *The Timeless Book on Leadership* (AuthorHouse, 2019), 198.
3. Brene Brown, quoted in Michelle Loch, *52 Weeks of Awesome Leadership.* (n.d.), 19, Lulu.com.

Transparency and Integrity

There is an undeniable link between transparency and trust. Transparency creates clarity and removes barriers to accessibility. With transparency, be prepared to answer more questions and concerns from those you lead. One last thought on transparency: It is perfectly fine to say to those you lead, "I do not know the answer to your question, but I will find out." Twenty-first-century leaders consistently demonstrate the characteristics of honesty and humility to those they lead. Consider this statement by leadership expert John C. Maxwell:

> Integrity means admitting it when you are wrong, putting others ahead of yourself, making decisions that may not be in your personal interest, fulfilling promises, and being genuine, humble and gracious. Trust is built on integrity. You cannot become a person of influence if people do not trust you.[4]

The word *integrity* comes from the Latin adjective *integer*, which means whole or complete. In my opinion, integrity in a remote work environment is one of the most critical soft skills a twenty-first-century leader should maintain. Unlike traditional brick-and-mortar work environments, remote work environments require a high level of integrity to ensure fidelity. It is not like you can just walk down the hallway and pop your head into the offices of those you lead remotely to make sure they are working. Core beliefs will serve as the foundational source of your philosophy and values, and those principles will shape your character and help to guide you along your journey in leadership.

---

4. John C. Maxwell and Jim Dornan, *Becoming a Person of Influence: How to Positively Impact the Lives of Others* (Nashville, TN: Thomas Nelson, Inc, 1997), E-book.

Character Is Foundational

Character is carved through life's lessons. The word *character* is derived from the Greek word *charattein*, which means to engrave. Have you experienced your fair share of adversity both personally and professionally? Growth is painful and yet a wonderful teacher of accountability. Stephen R. Covey had this to say about character: "Just as we develop our physical muscles through overcoming opposition—such as lifting weights—we develop our character muscles by overcoming challenges and adversity."[5]

I can remember, as a small child, getting caught telling a lie. My father would take me back to his room for an ethical discussion on decision-making, followed by swift punishment. Through the years and tears, my character was forged, and I am thankful that my parents loved me enough to hold me accountable for the choices I made and to teach me right from wrong. Hall of Fame coach John Wooden said it best: "Be more concerned with your character than your reputation, because your character is what you really are, while your reputation is merely what others think you are."[6]

Leaders Are Learners

Opening the door of influence requires both patience and persistence. Once open, a canvas full of opportunity is waiting for your imprint. Former president of the United States, the late John F. Kennedy said, "Leadership and learning are indispensable to each other."[7] Put simply, twenty-first-century leaders are learners. Never before in the history

---

5. Stephen Covey, quoted in A. Roger Merrill, Rebecca R. Merrill, and Stephen Covey, *First Things First Every Day: Daily Reflections—Because Where You're Headed Is More Important Than How Fast You Get There* (United Kingdom: Touchstone, 1997), 115.

6. John Wooden, quoted in Andy Zubko, *Treasury of Spiritual Wisdom: A Collection of 10,000 Powerful Quotations for Transforming Your Life* (India: Motilal Banarsidass Publishers Pvt. Limited, 2003), 51.

7. John F. Kennedy, quoted in *Connecting Leadership and Learning: Principles for Practice.* (Ukraine: Taylor & Francis, 2008), 32.

of the human race has knowledge been more readily available for consumption. Creating a culture of continual learning is one of the best investments a leader and an organization can make.

Twenty-first-century leaders understand that the world is dynamic and constantly changing. The difference between today's leader and a follower is like the difference between a thermometer and a thermostat. The thermometer will tell you what the temperature is. But the thermostat will, not only tell you what the temperature is, but also respond by turning on the heat or air-conditioning, which will, in turn, adjust the temperature to a comfortable climate. The ability to adapt or adjust is a necessary soft skill in the knowledge economy. There is a well-known Chinese proverb, which says that "the wise adapt themselves to circumstances, as water molds itself to the pitcher."

Self-directed learning within a collaborative and collegial ecosystem will foster the work environments of the future. By modeling a mindset of continual learning, you show those you lead that there is always room for improvement. The modern workplace is evolving. As new generations of leaders and followers make their way into the workforce, individuals who have surrendered to the status quo can very quickly find themselves marginalized through a form of Darwinian natural selection.

The twenty-first-century work environment is highly competitive, and survival belongs to the fittest. In the future, individuals will not only be competing with others for work but also with robots, known simply as "Bots." We will talk more about the future workplace in Chapter 12. What you need to know is that the middle class of the future will continue to be squeezed, and the knowledge gap will grow wider. This eventuality will necessitate continual learning not only to survive but to thrive in the work environment. One of the most important lessons a twenty-first-century leader can teach those they lead is to learn how to learn. Learning can occur in a variety of ways, but my favorite is by using the gradual release of responsibility model to empower those we lead.

Empowering Those You Lead to Lead

The gradual release of responsibility (GRR) model is a linear method of pedagogy framed around the process of devolving responsibility from the direct supervisor to the eventual independence of those they lead. The GRR model requires the direct supervisor to intentionally transition from having all the responsibility for performing a given task to enabling the direct reports to assume all the responsibility. Put simply, the sequence is *I do, we do, you do.* The leader gradually guides those they lead through scaffolding to the point of planned obsolescence. Individuals are unique and, as such, will be at different stages of development when you begin working with them. The key is to customize your leadership and meet them where they are and work toward a stage of independence.

Independence is a long-term play on behalf of the organization, and it is not without risk. Insecure twentieth-century leaders will struggle with giving up the traditional command and control, authoritarian type of leadership reminiscent of the industrial economy era. However, empowerment scales in a remote work environment. Do you want the people you lead to respect you? If so, you must respect them first. American psychiatrist Dr. Ari Kiev had this to say about respect:

> If you wish others to respect you, you must show respect for them. . . . Everyone wants to feel that he counts for something and is important to someone. Invariably, people will give their love, respect, and attention to the person who fills that need. Consideration for others generally reflects faith in self and faith in others.[8]

The old ways of using your authority or title to bully those you lead to maintain a sense of superiority are relics of the past. Those you lead will simply leave and find an organization that values their

---

8. Ari Kiev, quoted in John C. Maxwell and Jim Dornan, *How to Influence People: Make a Difference in Your World* (Nashville, TN: HarperCollins Leadership, 2013), E-book.

opinion and provides a supportive work environment. Twenty-first-century leaders view those they lead as partners in the process, not subordinates playing second fiddle. Author Stephen R. Covey summed up empowerment when he stated: "An empowered organization is one in which individuals have the knowledge, skill, desire, and opportunity to personally succeed in a way that leads to collective organizational success."[9] Remember, you can't lead if no one is following.

Focus on being a fountain, not a drain. John C. Maxwell writes, "When we learn to turn our focus from ourselves to others, the whole world opens up to us."[10] Do you know what your organization's greatest asset is? It's people. Therefore, twenty-first-century leaders must be servant leaders who understand that influence is the by-product of service. Leadership is the privilege that comes along when those you lead trust you to guide them on their journey. The people you lead want to make an impact and contribute to the greater good, so part of your job is to create the conditions for that to occur.

There is a direct correlation between employee engagement and organizational retention. Nurturing the next generation of leadership is the responsibility of a twenty-first-century leader. Winston Churchill said, "We make a living by what we get; we make a life by what we give."[11] Do you want to increase your scope of influence? Start by mentoring and coaching someone on your team who shows both potential and promise. Creating a culture of coaching:

- Creates synergy within your team or department
- Increases employee satisfaction
- Builds a continuous feedback loop for improvement

9. Stephen R. Covey, *Principle-Centered Leadership* (United Kingdom: Free Press, 2003), 212.

10. John C. Maxwell, *Everyone Communicates, Few Connect: What the Most Effective People Do Differently* (New York: HarperCollins, 2010), 35.

11. Winston Churchill, quoted in Judith Glaser, *42 Rules for Creating WE: A Hands-On, Practical Approach to Organizational Development, Change and Leadership Best Practices,* 2nd ed. (Cupertino, CA: Superstar Press, 2009), E-book.

- Aligns your employees' goals with your organization's priorities
- Reduces employee attrition

Employee engagement occurs when your employees' priorities intersect with your organization's priorities. Of course, priorities are unique and vary from one employee to another. Some individuals may be motivated by increased compensation, while others are motivated by a healthy work-life balance. Therefore, leaders must identify and answer two questions with those they lead: Why are you here? How do you define success? The answer to these two questions creates clarity for the twenty-first-century leader and allows them to identify the common denominator between individual wants and organizational needs. Author John C. Maxwell has one of the best definitions of success I have seen. He believes that "success is knowing your purpose in life, growing to reach your maximum potential, and sowing seeds that benefit others."[12] Employee engagement is a result of a symbiotic relationship between giving and getting.

Establishing employee engagement is not the end goal. Sustaining employee engagement is what differentiates great organizations from good organizations. This naturally leads one to ask: How do we maintain a high level of employee engagement and maximize our organization's potential to succeed? The answer is that we do so through coordination. Sharing responsibility allows individuals and organizations to align individual skills with organizational goals. Tapping into the talents of those you lead creates synergy and allows for growth and development to occur over the long term, resulting in a culture of shared collaboration and coordination.

Leaders bolster engagement by consistently connecting individual passions to organizational priorities. Motivating those you lead is a necessary step that twenty-first-century leaders use to sustain employee engagement. In *Start with Why*, Simon Sinek says, "People don't buy

---

12. Maxwell, *Your Road Map to Success*, 11.

What you do, they buy Why you do it."[13] Your why is your organization's purpose. Purpose is derived from your organization's values. Values should be aligned with your organization's mission statement. Alignment creates balance, and balance creates congruence within your team and organization.

Twenty-first-century leaders understand what fuels individual ambitions is to find meaning and purpose in life. Great leaders create clarity and a sense of direction for the teams they lead. Both meaning and purpose are found when a group of individuals becomes committed to a goal bigger than themselves, a more significant cause if you will, that allows them to contribute and thus maximize their potential. Businessman Andrew Carnegie observed that "teamwork is the ability to work together toward a common vision. The ability to direct individual accomplishments toward organizational objectives. It is the fuel that allows common people to attain uncommon results."[14]

Consistent deposits of time in a one-on-one environment will allow your influence to grow with those you lead. Time is to influence what water is to a garden. By consistently pouring into those you lead, growth from seed to plant will occur in the form of cooperation. Cooperation is consent to collaborate, and voluntary cooperation from those you lead is the key to unlock the door of influence.

---

13. Simon Sinek, *Start with Why: How Great Leaders Inspire Everyone to Take Action* (United Kingdom: Penguin Publishing Group, 2009), 41.
14. Andrew Carnegie, quoted in David DeFord, *1000 Brilliant Achievement Quotes: Advice from the World's Wisest*, 2nd ed. (Scotts Valley, CA: CreateSpace Independent Publishing Platform, 2004), 185.

Change

Change your thoughts and you change your world.

—Norman Vincent Peale

I should begin this chapter with a disclaimer: if you are a first-generation leader or a leader who struggles with embracing change, you may find Chapter 3 a little heavy on leadership theory and abstract concepts. If you find your mind begins to wander, I want to encourage you to put this book down and take a break. But don't give up on it. The leadership theory presented here is critical to laying a basic foundation for understanding human behavior. And only by developing a comprehensive understanding of human behavior can we better understand ourselves and others.

When I became a leader, I made the mistake of believing my job was to make people happy. I followed a policy of appeasement, and my barometer of the job that I was doing was contingent on the happiness of those that I was leading. If they were unhappy with their circumstances or with me for that matter, I would try even harder to please them. John C. Maxwell said: "When you realize that people treat you according to how they see themselves rather than how you really are, you are less likely to be affected by their behavior."[1] I mistakenly believed that if the people I led were happy, I must be doing a good job. Boy, was I wrong. My flawed belief continued until one day I talked with my father who had been in leadership roles for most of his life. I was explaining to him my frustration over the lack of progress with those I was leading in my new leadership role and how exhausting it was. My father very calmly put his hand on my shoulder and said, "Bart, if you try to please everyone, you'll end up pleasing no one." I stood there speechless and realized that if I was going to change my circumstances, the first person who needed to change was me.

Embracing Change

The only constant in this life is change. So, you have two options, evolve or get passed by. Throughout recent human history, change—or what we like to call progress—has been a staple in every industrial economy. Pause for a minute and think about some of the changes you have seen in your lifetime: from wired phones to smartphones, from stationary desktops to mobile laptops, from dial-up to high-speed internet—the world has changed. We have moved from the industrial age into the information age where the answers to our questions are simply on-demand and at the touch of a button. Yet a portion of society continues to cling to the security of silos; such industrial-age thinking is terminal. The traditional four walls of business and industry are being torn down by a digital revolution, which has flattened the world into a high-tech globalized or collaborative economy.

The digital transformation is here; it is not going away, and it demands that we change or get left behind. Consequently, nonprofit and for-profit organizations around the globe are scrambling to keep up with global competition and the rapid speed of change in the twenty-first century. A focus on productivity and efficiency has forced most

---

1. John C. Maxwell, *Be a People Person: Effective Leadership Through Effective Relationships* (Colorado Springs, CO: David C Cook, 2013), 130.

organizations to innovate and think outside the box when it comes to hiring employees. For example, organizations around the globe are considering whether to hire the most talented individuals within a radius of their brick-and-mortar facilities or whether they should shift their paradigm and hire the most talented individuals regardless of location. The latter creates what is commonly referred to as a virtual or remote work environment.

Your competition is counting on a countenance of inertia within your organization. Inertia is defined as the resistance of any physical object to any change in its velocity. Isaac Newton summarized in his first law of motion that an object not subject to any net external force moves at a constant velocity. Thus, an object will continue moving at its current velocity until some force causes its speed or direction to change.

Progress is not possible without change. The challenge is that we have a natural tendency to want to avoid change and become rigid in our thinking. This mental rigidity is referred to as psychosclerosis. Psychosclerosis is the hardening of the attitude and the mind to a point where we can become unteachable. If we allow psychosclerosis to take hold in our minds, we stop growing and developing. We stop evolving. This mindset creates a self-perpetuating paralysis by analysis.

Leaders Must Be Innovators

To allow innovation to take root, organizations and leaders must be intentional about creating a safe space where those they lead can experiment and make mistakes in the name of progress. Learning can be linear, and failure is part of the process. To be successful, leaders must embrace the process and create intentional space for those they lead to innovate and observe.

Twenty-first-century leaders are innovators; they are disruptors of the status quo in their respective fields. These leaders like to think outside the box and answer the what-if questions. Innovators are idealists at their core; they are pioneers who have an insatiable appetite for improvement.

For most organizations, the challenge lies not in the idea behind innovation but actually in the adoption of change. Adoption usually starts with the recognition that a need exists. Apple cofounder Steve Jobs once said that "innovation distinguishes between a leader and a follower."[2] The rate of adoption in your organization will typically follow a bell curve, which can best be described by a theory known as the Diffusion of Innovations. This theory tries to explain how, why, and at what rate new ideas and technology spread. Sociologist Everett Rogers promoted the concept in his book *Diffusion of Innovations*. The theory has been applied across a multitude of fields, including medicine, sociology, and education. Rogers suggests there are five categories of adopters:[3]

1.   Innovators
2.   Early Adopters
3.   Early Majority
4.   Late Majority
5.   Laggards

Innovators are disruptors of the status quo; innovators have a high-risk tolerance and are not afraid to fail. Facebook cofounder Mark Zuckerberg had this to say about risk: "The biggest risk is not taking any risk. In a world that is changing quickly, the only strategy that is guaranteed to fail is not taking risks."[4] Innovators understand that with risk comes reward. They represent only 2.5% of your organization. Typically, innovators are pioneers in their field and are willing to lead the charge into unknown territory. Some examples of innovators that you may have heard of include Jeff Bezos, Steve Jobs, Elon Musk, Bill Gates, and Sam Walton.

---

2. Steve Jobs, quoted in Wes Husted, *7 Things You Should Know About Being a Leader*, Janet Angelo, ed. (Indiego Publishing LLC, 2014), 18.
3. Everett M. Rogers, *Diffusion of Innovations*, 5th ed. (United Kingdom: Free Press, 2003).
4. Mark Zuckerberg, quoted in Don M. Chance, *Financial Risk Management: An End User Perspective* (Singapore: World Scientific Publishing Company, 2019), 35.

Early adopters are a bit more methodical in their adoption of change. They see the value in adopting innovation but are more prudent in their choices. Early adopters believe the old saying that "the early bird gets the worm, but the second mouse gets the cheese." Did you catch that? That was my attempt at humor. Early adopters are essential to your organization's success because, by word of mouth, they generate the social momentum necessary for the majority to accept change. They are the influencers in your leadership ecosystem; early adopters represent roughly 13.5% of your organization.

The early majority sit on what I call the fence of apathy. They are cautious and slow to embrace change, but they represent the first prodigious segment of the organization to embrace change. The early majority are followers disguised as leaders within your organization. They tend to flock with other individuals in the early majority and adopt change when they feel it is safe to do so. This group represents approximately 34% of your organization; they will accept change once they see either innovators or early adopters achieving success.

The late majority are skeptics of change and represent roughly 34% of your organization. The late majority are the last significant sector of your organization to adopt an innovative mindset. These individuals are typically older, risk-averse, and set in their ways. The late majority are procrastinators; they will accept change, but only if they are forced to.

Laggards are the last group in your organization to adopt innovation. Laggards represent the final 16% of your organization's population. They are resistors to change—traditionalists at their core. A laggard would rather use a typewriter than a computer. A laggard would prefer to use a landline telephone than a cellular phone. A laggard would rather write handwritten letters than use email. Are you getting the picture? As a twenty-first-century leader, you should spend little to no time trying to convince this group to adopt change. In the highly competitive workforce of the twenty-first century, laggards will be the first group in your organization to lose their jobs due to a lack of malleability.

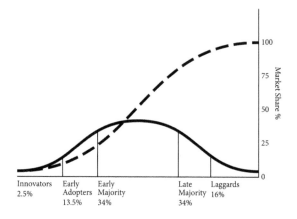

Innovators 2.5%	Early Adopters 13.5%	Early Majority 34%		Late Majority 34%	Laggards 16%

Creating Momentum

Successful change requires energy and enthusiasm. Fortunately, enthusiasm is contagious. Author Bryant H. McGill says that "enthusiasm is the energy and force that builds literal momentum of the human soul and mind."[5] One of my favorite metaphors to describe momentum is the flywheel.

The *flywheel effect* was a term used by author Jim Collins in *Good to Great*. The flywheel is a circular device designed to store rotational energy efficiently. I want you to begin to see the individuals you lead as stored energy, full of potential. The question you must ask is this: How do I unlock that stored energy and help those I lead to maximize their potential? There is a terrific TED Talk titled "The Flywheel Effect" by Edgar D. Barron that provides in-depth insight to this metaphor.

Dr. Barron suggests that an energy source is harmless without something or someone to ignite it. The flywheel represents those you lead. Starting the flywheel begins at the base with experience. Dr. Barron believes that "experience is really the process by which we see and we know, it's the way that we make sense of information around us,

---

5. Bryant H. McGill, quoted in James Frey, *Words to Live By: Concepts, Ideas, and Values for Your Life* (Carlsbad, CA: Balboa Press, 2018).

it's the way that we process our input."[6] What we have experienced as leaders will determine what we ultimately see as possible.

Possibility represents the second tier of the flywheel. Once we understand and believe that something is possible, then we're able to act on what we see. According to Dr. Barron, "Your ability to act is reinforced and is relegated to your subconscious based on what you see as possible because of your experiences."[7]

Next, action rests at the apex of the flywheel; it is at this point that those you lead have to choose whether to act or not act. Dr. Barron suggests that inaction is just a symptom and could be a result of those you lead not having the necessary experience to determine what is possible. Are some of the individuals that you lead not maximizing their potential? Perhaps they lack organizational experience, which leads to self-doubt, which fuels the inaction both you and your organization are currently experiencing.

Action leads to results, which is the fourth tier of the flywheel. Dr. Barron suggests that "once we act on what we believe is possible, then we get results from our actions."[8] Results are the by-product of cohesive action, and they will define your leadership. Your results shape your experience, which determines what is possible, allowing those you lead to take action that leads to the results both you and your organization desire.

Action

Possible   Results

Experience

6. Edgar D. Barron, "The Flywheel Effect," TED Talk, May 7, 2015, https://youtu.be/JLj5hCmNovk.
7. Barron, "Flywheel Effect."
8. Barron, "Flywheel Effect."

You might be asking yourself what to do if those I lead don't have a reservoir of experience to draw from? Lack of experience is not uncommon in a rapidly growing twenty-first-century economy. The challenge in a rapid growth organization is that many times, the individuals you are leading lack the necessary experience to start the flywheel or to handle the inevitable problems that will arise. Leaders must fill this shallow reservoir with expertise that can provide both context and perspective.

Dr. Barron suggests that these individuals will have to "borrow" from your experience until they can complete one cycle of the flywheel. Their results will inform their experience, and they will have a pool of perspective from which to draw moving forward. What is critical in rapid growth work environments is that expectations and communication are clear and consistent for all new employees. This clarity creates confidence in the change of direction toward disruptive innovation.

Disruptive innovation lies at the heart of the twenty-first-century economy. The term was coined by Professor Clayton M. Christensen and his collaborators in 1995. A disruptive innovation is one that produces a new market by providing a different set of values, which ultimately and quickly overwhelm an existing market. Has your profession or market been disrupted during your lifetime?

Some examples of disruptive innovation in my lifetime include the shift from personal computers to smartphones in the computing industry, vinyl records to eight-track tapes to cassette tapes to compact discs to digital music in the music industry, DVDs and video rental to digital streaming in the video industry, automobiles fueled by gasoline to vehicles powered by electricity, and newspapers to social media outlets in the publishing world. The common denominator in each example is new technology emerging and challenging the current way of thinking.

Technology is continuing to create a digital storm by converging on industries in a constantly evolving and competitive landscape. Therefore, organizations must become living organisms, resisting complacency and responding with a growth mindset. Pope Paul VI said:

> All life demands struggle. Those who have everything given to them become lazy, selfish, and insensitive to the real values of life. The very striving and hard work that we so constantly try to avoid is the major building block in the person we are today.[9]

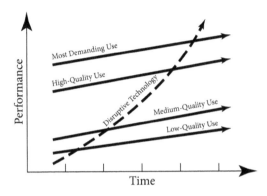

Customized Individual Development Plans

For organizations to function at their maximum potential, leaders need to focus their development efforts on customizing a personalized growth and development plan that includes asynchronous training, synchronous shadowing, and one-on-one coaching. Individuals want and need a personalized growth and development plan that is relevant to the role they will play in the organization. Therefore, training should encompass both a micro and macro perspective. The micro includes the specifics of the person's position followed by clear expectations of what is to be completed on a daily or weekly basis. The more quantifiable your organization can make the job, the more efficiently you can track the

---

9. Pope Paul VI, quoted in Bruce Schultz, *The Passion Filled Life: Make Living Your Passion* (Parker, CO: Outskirts Press, 2019), 83.

progress of your remote work employees. Progress should be monitored and discussed weekly through ongoing and sustained group meetings between the leader and the individuals they lead. The macro involves the mission statement, organizational values, and understanding the why behind the vision of your organization.

Synchronous shadowing opportunities should be designed to provide meaningful experiences and conversations. The term *synchronous* means simultaneous. Synchronous shadowing provides intentional opportunities for those you lead to begin networking with their peers and also helps to break down barriers that can form in a remote work environment. Synchronous shadowing can provide context to those you lead by allowing them to experience the organization from a different angle. Reflection and takeaways should be discussed after synchronous shadowing opportunities through one-on-one coaching. Let's talk coaching in Chapter 4.

Culture of Coaching

Remember, you don't have to know it all to be a great leader!
Be yourself. People would rather follow a leader who is
always real than one who is always right.

—Craig Groeschel

I am a former head basketball coach. When I began working as a virtual leader, I was struck by two things. First, there were no rules when it came to virtual leadership. The landscape was new and unpaved. Very little research had been done nationally on leading individuals in a remote work environment. In the absence of structure and a template to follow, I decided to create my own blueprint. The second thing that struck me was how similar the problems I was facing in a virtual work environment were to the challenges I had faced as a head basketball coach. From a lack of communication to a lack of execution, the individuals I supervised did not always function as a team. Many of them were operating in silos and lacked a commitment to work cooperatively and consistently with others. They were talented but lacked patience and a collective purpose. So, I decided to lay a solid foundation by creating a culture of coaching within the organization. My goal was to help every person I led to begin to discover their why.

Remember Your Why

By starting with why, organizations can define their purpose, which is the DNA of an organization. The next generation of employees are searching not just for work but for meaningful work. To be effective, leaders need to have a high emotional intelligence quotient (EQ). The initial (EQ) question for growing organizations and leaders to ask is: Do we need to rightsize our employee-supervisor ratios? Rightsizing your organization's ratios allows for meaningful relationships to form. A good ratio for virtual leaders to consistently maintain is seven employees to one supervisor. The seven-to-one ratio allows for coaching to occur at regular intervals.

Have you been to a basketball game lately? I can remember when I used to be a basketball coach; I always tried to have seven to eight players I could count on every night when we went into battle. The depth would give me some margin if one of my starters got into foul trouble or if another starter got hurt. I also knew we had players coming off the bench who could execute and operate effectively in crunch time because I had spent a sufficient amount of time teaching them in practice and coaching them in previous games. Quality ratios lead to positive and cohesive team chemistry. In over 20 years of working in a variety of leadership capacities, I have learned that individuals are unique; they come equipped with emotions, aspirations, and needs. You might be asking yourself: How do I identify the needs of those I lead? The answer is simple—by asking questions and taking the time to listen. Remember, before your direct reports buy into your vision, they buy into your heart.

Cultivate Your Team

There is power in diversity. Great leaders respect the differences of those they lead. One of my favorite sayings is that "the rainbow is full of different colors for a reason." If it was all the same color, the rainbow would not be nearly as beautiful. High EQ leaders embrace alternative viewpoints; they realize that discussion coupled with respectful debate is healthy and provides a necessary check and balance for the team. Employees who feel that they are consistently heard and who believe that their opinion is valued and respected rarely leave.

Employee recruiting and retention will continue to be highly competitive in the twenty-first century. In his best-selling book *Good to Great*, Jim Collins talks about getting the right people on the bus and getting the wrong people off the bus.[1] Does your organization have the right people on the bus? The key to organizational alignment is to start with who, not what. Intrinsically motivated, self-starting employees thrive in the autonomy of a remote work environment because they feel empowered by the trust granted and encouraged by the space to be innovative.

Empowerment is a by-product of trust. One way that virtual leaders can earn trust is by modeling values that construct the core framework on which integrity resides. What are your values? Virtual leaders will be judged on two primary attributes: competence and character. In my opinion, adhering to values is essential in a remote work environment; by modeling values and then consistently reinforcing them with those you lead, the result is buy-in.

Are the people who directly report to you buying what you're selling? When your direct reports choose to follow your lead, they relinquish control and become pliable and can be influenced. Once the bridge of influence has been crossed, leaders must be mindful that their words have weight. Choose your words carefully because you never know who is listening.

The nucleus of innovation is creativity and, therefore, leaders focus on what-if. A what-if mentality embraces the unpredictability of the twenty-first-century economy. Having the creativity to reimagine both problems and solutions allows for innovation to take root as the winds of change continue to blow.

---

1. Jim Collins, *Good to Great: Why Some Companies Make the Leap and Others Don't* (United Kingdom: Random House Business, 2001).

Create a Culture of Coaching

Creating a culture of coaching in your organization is necessary to keep pace with the unpredictable landscape of the twenty-first century. Leaders activate and drive innovation with those they lead by creating a safe and open ecosystem of support that allows rapid experimentation and exploration to take shape. Abraham Maslow believed that "in any given moment we have two options: to step forward into growth or step back into safety."[2] Stepping forward will require guidance in the form of mentors. However, where most organizations miss the mark is that the typical corporate mentoring program is nothing more than a transactional experience. When it comes to training employees, you can't reproduce what you don't have. If there is very little depth or consistency in the training of new employees, you are wasting your time. A culture of coaching allows for sustained mentoring to take place throughout and beyond the initial employee orientation. Mentoring is where your direct reports begin to connect the dots.

I can remember connecting the dots as a rookie teacher and first-year head basketball coach. The year was 1998, and I had been assigned a mentor teacher to help walk me through my first year in public education. Coach Armstrong was a longtime basketball coach at Eufaula High School. As winter approached, the weather in Oklahoma had grown colder. One round of snow had fallen, and a mixture of sleet and rain began to fall. Because of the inclement weather, I had parked my vehicle in a no-parking zone wanting to get as close to the basketball gym as I could. As I was visiting with some fellow coaches in the gym, Coach Armstrong came in, screaming at me for creating my own parking space. He said, "Don't you know you are parked in a fire zone?" Before I could respond, Coach Armstrong said, "If the principal comes down here and finds you parked in a fire zone, he is going to go ballistic. He could get in a lot of trouble for that. You need to go move your car now."

---

2. Abraham Maslow, quoted in Bruce Schultz, *The Passion Filled Life: Make Living Your Passion* (Denver, CO: Outskirts Press, 2019), 232.

Sheepishly, I said okay. What you need to know is that the parking lot at Eufaula High School was created with about a 45-degree angle to help with drainage and running water. As I stepped outside into the drizzle, I could see that the parking lot was full of student vehicles, and the only parking spots available were down the hill at the very bottom of the parking lot near the entrance. Not wanting to get in trouble as a new teacher and coach, I backed my car up into the snow and began to make my way down the steep decline to the entry or bottom of the parking area. After parking, I stepped out of my vehicle, and by then, it was pouring rain. I began my march up the incline to the gymnasium, and as soon as I reached the top, I saw Coach Armstrong pull his diesel truck into my original parking spot. In shock and disbelief, I turned and could see all my coaching friends roaring with laughter at me through the glass window in the lobby of the gymnasium. Coach Armstrong taught me a couple of valuable lessons that day. Lesson 1: don't park in a fire zone. Lesson 2: there are some lessons only experience can teach.

Set SMART Goals

American businessman Bo Bennett said, "A dream becomes a goal when action is taken toward its achievement."[3] Successful coaches create clarity by helping those they lead to identify the outcome they desire. Setting goals begins with a dream. What would you love to do? If I guaranteed that you could accomplish any goal you set, what would you be willing to try? Children are a beautiful example of the ability to dream. If you ask a toddler what they want to be when they grow up, the sky's the limit. American businessman and motivational speaker Les Brown said, "Too many of us are not living our dreams because we are living our fears."[4] The next step in the sequence is to speak your dreams into existence and document your goals.

---

3. Bo Bennett, quoted in Noelle Federico and J. Allan Jones, *Practical Change: 8 Ways to Rejuvenate Your Life* (Brentwood, TN: Music City News Publishing, 2005), 15.

4. Les Brown, quoted in Dave Ramsey, *EntreLeadership: 20 Years of Practical Business Wisdom from the Trenches* (United Kingdom: Howard Books, 2011), 60.

Before every New Year's Eve, I will sit down with my family and discuss our individual goals for the upcoming year. Writing goals down or typing them into a document that is saved takes the intangible and makes it tangible. Your goals are your guide along the journey to leadership maturation. Now I want you to prioritize your goals into two buckets: short term and long term. Short-term goals are goals that you can achieve in 12 months or less; whereas long-term goals are goals that take more than 12 months to complete. Once you have determined which bucket your goals belong in, take a minute to make sure that each one of your goals is objective. I use the acronym SMART to help me make sure that my goals lack subjectivity. SMART stands for:

- Specific
- Measurable
- Attainable
- Realistic
- Timely

SMART goals start with specific areas in need of improvement. The objective needs to be measurable to quantify or at least demonstrate an indicator of progress. Your goals should be attainable and within reach. Realistic goals are reasonable, given the available resources. Timely goals have a timeline that specifies when the goals are to be met. The final step in the goal-setting process is to share your goals with your direct supervisor. Verbalizing your goals will allow your immediate supervisor to help hold you accountable for achieving the results you desire. Accountability creates discipline, and discipline is the conduit to the achievement of your goals.

Helping those you lead to accomplish both personal and professional goals will require direction. Coaches are like the Sherpas of the Himalayas. The Sherpas are native to some of the most mountainous regions of Tibet. Sherpas are highly skilled mountain climbers with experience ascending incredibly mountainous terrain that includes snow, glacial ice, and rock. Sherpas are also known for their ability to keep those they are leading as safe as possible by mitigating risk. Sherpas know the most efficient way to navigate those they are leading to the peak of the mountain. Remember, the journey always begins by identifying a direction.

Coaches take action by charting the course. Preparing those you lead for the expedition your team is about to take begins with a proactive mindset. Often, leaders fail to plan and predetermine a direction; inevitably, when the winds of change begin to blow, the team is blown off course and into scramble or reactive mode. The result forces a reactionary mindset whereby those you lead waste time troubleshooting, overcoming obstacles, and putting out fires. Great coaches are always a step ahead and have the ability to make course corrections on the fly.

CHAPTER 5

Self-Awareness

The unexamined life is not worth living.

—Socrates

Handling Leadership Blind Spots

Blind spots are characteristics in your leadership style, of which you are unaware, that limit your ability to influence others. The good news is that blind spots in your leadership can and improve through awareness. Let me share a few of my past blind spots:

1. Avoiding conflict and not having tough conversations.
2. Flying solo and failing to ask for help.
3. Lacking emotional intelligence (EQ) and sensitivity toward those I lead.
4. Playing the blame game and perpetuating a victim mentality.
5. Accepting and adopting low standards.

Understanding and embracing our blind spots is the first step in resolving what psychologists refer to as cognitive dissonance. Cognitive dissonance is a psychological stress experienced by someone who simultaneously holds two or more contradictory ideas, beliefs, or values.

The tension is caused by new evidence that challenges the person's established assumptions. Humans strive for internal congruence, so our mental makeup sets out to resolve the conflict and return to a harmonious pattern of thinking. As the saying goes: so within, so without.

Addressing blind spots creates clarity and confidence in those you lead. Uncertainty is contagious, and it can result in timidity in decision-making. Virtual leaders understand this and strive to model courage and confidence to those they lead. The key to self-confidence is maintaining a healthy balance. Too much confidence and those you lead will describe you as arrogant; too little confidence and those you lead will define you as timid. Leaders who remain balanced, cerebral, and optimistic during difficult times demonstrate resilience or grit to those they lead.

Grit is the ability to sustain passion and persistence over an extended period of time. In my opinion, grit is another one of the Top 10 soft skills needed to thrive in a twenty-first-century economy. One of my favorite quotes is from actor and director Woody Allen, who said that "80% of success is showing up."[1] Research studies have shown a correlation between high achievement and grit. Challenges are inevitable in the workplace of the future, but it is the ability to consistently overcome challenges that separates the winners from the losers. As we learned in Chapter 1, talent is innate, but grit can be developed over time. Consider this statement from author and psychologist Angela Duckworth: "Grit is a better predictor of achievement than intellectual talent (IQ), because grit serves as the overriding factor that provides the stamina required to 'stay the course' amid challenges and setbacks."[2]

---

1. Woody Allen, quoted in *Harvard Business Review on Advancing Your Career* (Harvard Business Review Press, 2011), 166.
2. Wikipedia s.v. "Grit (Personality Trait)," last modified June 3, 2020, https://en.wikipedia.org/wiki/Grit_(personality_trait).

How Coaching Improves Awareness

Creating a culture of coaching in your organization shifts leaders' focus from authority to awareness. Great coaches are conscientious and patient; they have the innate ability to separate the major from the minor when it comes to conflict and adversity. At their core, successful coaches are problem solvers. In commenting on problems, American author Norman Vincent Peale had this to say: "Every problem has in it the seeds of its own solution. If you don't have any problems, you don't get any seeds."[3] I too believe that every problem has a solution; although we may not know what the solution is at this time, there is always an answer.

Coaches don't simply give answers to every question. Sometimes, they teach those they lead to find their answers. What separates human beings from the robots of the future workforce is the ability to empathize. We will talk more about the future in Chapter 12. The problems of the twenty-first-century economy are complex. Exceptional coaches embrace sophistication through simplification. Simplify for those you lead down to the least common denominator by starting with a question. My favorite questions to ask always begin with *why*. What I want you to know is that creative solutions intended to improve performance always require abstract thinking.

Virtual Competition, Cooperation, and Collaboration

Performance is what separates good leaders from great leaders. Author Brian Tracy expressed it this way: "The true measure of the value of any business leader and manager is performance."[4] The ability to produce provides evidence of progress and builds trust within your organization that you can achieve the goals that have been set. The genesis of performance begins with ownership or full responsibility for

---

3. Norman Vincent Peale, quoted in John Mason, *Know Your Limits—Then Ignore Them* (Tulsa, OK: Insight Publishing Group, 1999), 140.
4. Brian Tracy, quoted in Dr. Pierre Casse, *Handy Notes for the Busy Leaders: Reflections on Leadership-in-Action* (United Kingdom: Xlibris, 2018), Kindle.

the outcomes of those you lead. I have a battle cry with those I lead: No excuses, No regrets, Total Ownership!

The road to success is paved with high standards, which Ray Kroc characterized this way: "The quality of a leader is reflected in the standards they set for themselves."[5] Remote work environments require the individuals you lead to set a high standard of excellence for themselves. Individual standards of excellence create a consistent barometer of expectations to be met. Creating a culture whereby individuals hold themselves accountable is the secret sauce for generating sustained performance. Once individual standards have been solidified, it is time to raise the bar by creating a healthy culture of competition and cooperation.

Winning coaches understand that the driving force behind success in the future is the ability to adapt or evolve. This mental malleability allows organizations of the future to remain agile and adaptive to the changing landscape of the twenty-first century. Virtual competition is a derivative of individuals who coexist in a remote work environment. However, virtual competition left unchecked and lacking balance can become toxic to the work environment. Leaders must mix virtual competition and virtual cooperation into a soup of virtual collaboration.

Virtual cooperation is the process by which individuals work together to achieve a common goal. Coaches understand the sum is always greater than its parts. Yet another ingredient in creating a cooperative virtual work environment is the need to develop a virtual community. Virtual communities are a necessary part of the remote work environment. A virtual community is a small social unit in which the members have something in common. In some cases, it may refer to employees who are in the same department or who were hired the same year. Virtual communities come in all shapes and sizes. Commonalities can be based on factors such as geography, job title, or skill set. These commu-

---

5. Ray Kroc, quoted in Kim Olver, *Empowered Leadership: How to Get the Best from Your Team* (Chicago, IL: Inside Out Press, 2008), Kindle.

nities provide support through sharing information, and they can create opportunities to develop synergy and solidarity among coworkers.

Virtual work communities of the future will communicate using synchronous and asynchronous communication. Remember, synchronous communication means simultaneous or occurring at the same time. Asynchronous is just the opposite of synchronous and is communication that is not live or simultaneous. Both are necessary in a remote work environment for differing reasons.

Virtual work environments can create feelings of isolation and segregation. Consistent synchronous communication opportunities are necessary to foster a symbiotic sense of teamwork and togetherness. Asynchronous communication is also required to develop the imaginary boundaries necessary to complete one's daily tasks. Time is ubiquitous in a remote work environment, so it becomes essential to create some soft boundaries to deter the inevitable distractions throughout the workday.

Measuring to Ensure Transparency and Accountability

Reciprocal accountability is necessary in a remote work environment. If I can see your data and you can see mine, the result is openness and flow of information. Initially, your direct reports may be slow to warm up to the idea of 360-degree transparency, but over time they will grow to appreciate the structure. Disclosing information openly to all stakeholders creates clarity and mitigates miscommunication. Disclosure establishes a culture of accountability that fosters maturity among stakeholders, ensuring that individuals own their data, whether good or bad.

What gets measured gets done. Calculating progress or measuring is essential to maintaining momentum. In a virtual work environment, the mean becomes the standard by which all employees are measured in your department. I call this process bumping the mean. Transparency creates the conditions whereby those you lead can hold themselves accountable. The mean creates a dynamic goal that increases incrementally over time if your organization is making progress toward its stated objectives.

I have found there are many ways to measure progress, but the one I find most valuable is what I call the Third Dimension. The Third Dimension is a quick and easy way to discern progress or lack thereof versus the mean. Individual team members can hold themselves accountable by bumping their numbers against the mean. Likewise, the leader can hold those they lead accountable by using the mean as the standard by which team members are measured. By taking your data through three layers or filters, you can determine whether you have a disconnect, starting with Layer 1.

An excellent metaphor for Layer 1 is the game of golf. One of the things I love most about golf is that you can compete against yourself. A golfer's number of strokes on a hole, course, or tournament is compared to the par score. The score is recorded either as the number that the golfer was over or under par. Layer 1 of the Third Dimension is *you versus yourself*. For our purposes, par is the mean. Contingent upon how often your reporting is available (daily, weekly, monthly, quarterly, semiannually, or annually), you calculate the mean or par and simply ask yourself: Did I make progress from one reporting window to the next? If the answer is yes, you celebrate the achievement, but if the answer is no, you move to the second layer.

Layer 2 of the Third Dimension is *you versus your tribal mean*. Calculating your colleagues' mean into a cumulative team average and sharing this data transparently gives you a pulse on how you are performing against your peers who have received the same communication from the same direct supervisor that you did. I call this positive peer pressure. Sam Walton, the founder of Walmart, once said, "High expectations are the key to everything."[6] Those you lead will

---

6. Sam Walton, quoted in Timothy Baldwin, Bill Bommer, and Robert Rubin, *Developing Management Skills: What Great Managers Know and Do* (New York: McGraw-Hill Education, 2007), 245.

rise and fall to the level of your expectations. The tribal mean is a fair standard because it represents the sum of the numbers divided by how many numbers are being averaged. Simply ask yourself: Is my mean above my tribal mean? If the answer is yes, you celebrate the progress, but if the answer is no, you move to the third layer.

Layer 3 of the Third Dimension is *you versus your departmental mean*. Large organizations are constructed with multiple layers to reduce ratios and raise accountability. Calculating your departmental mean into a cumulative organizational average creates an aggregated indicator for those you lead to hold themselves accountable. Macro indicators are the cleanest data you have because the large number of factors in the equation makes it difficult for an individual to skew or manipulate the numbers. Again, ask yourself: Is my mean above my departmental mean? If the answer is yes, you rejoice, but if the answer is no, you have a disconnect. Disconnects require those you lead to do a deep dive and answer this question: Why did I fail to make progress from one reporting window to the next? As they say, the devil is in the details. Dig into your data to discern the disconnect.

One last bit of advice on the mean. Beware of regression to the mean. In leadership, regression to the mean is the phenomenon that if a number is extreme on its first measurement, it will tend to be closer to the average on its second measurement. If the number is extreme on the second measurement, it will more than likely have been closer to the average on its first. Metrics should be measured consistently over time. Sustained analysis takes into account statistical anomalies that can deviate from the mean.

Look at your organization's competitive season as a marathon, not a sprint. I am told that there are two critical times in any marathon. The first is at the start of the race. The pace that is set when the starting gun fires is a vital component of any marathon. One of the biggest challenges that many marathoners face is starting too fast and then fading in the later portions of the race. Others begin with too slow a pace and find themselves playing catch-up the rest of the race. The second critical time for any runner is the halfway point. The halfway point is a great time to measure the progress or regression of those you lead.

Excellence is not an accident. American historian Will Durant said, "We are what we repeatedly do. Excellence, then, is not an act, but a habit." Let me give you a few successful habits I have observed in influential virtual leaders; they have the ability to:

1. Grind – Grinders show up every day and outperform colleagues with more talent through hard work and determination.
2. Share the Credit – Affirmation sings to the soul and demonstrates humility to those you lead.
3. Accept Feedback – Communication is the currency of achievement.

Virtual leadership is about managing your organization's objectives in a harmonious sequence through synchronous and asynchronous means using the resources you have to perform at your maximum potential. Consider this statement by American author Clayton M. Christensen:

> Management is getting people together to figure out how to transform inputs into outputs. In the process of figuring out the process of how people work together, you've got to figure out who's got what responsibilities, and how do they work together.[7]

The key is coordination, but how we achieve coordination has more to do with our methods of management than any other skill set.

Choosing the Right Leadership Style

Leadership style is inherent but can also be a learned attribute. Let's discuss two primary leadership styles to see where you fall on the

---

7. Clayton M. Christensen, quoted in Bert Forschelen, *Compendium of Quotes for Entrepreneurs and Managers* (Germany: Gabler Publishing House, 2017), E-book.

leadership continuum. The first leadership style is authoritarian—sometimes referred to as autocratic leadership. Autocratic leaders maintain full control of the direction of those they lead with minimal input. Authoritarian leaders provide nominal autonomy with a strict focus on the achievement of the stated objectives. Autocratic leadership is challenging in a virtual work environment because it requires supervision at all times to maintain course, and the leader does not share the same physical space with those they lead.

The second leadership style is democratic. Democratic leadership promotes equity in decision-making. Democratic leaders believe the sum is always greater than its parts. This type of leadership believes in two-way communication and sharing control of the direction the group or tribe takes. Autonomy is earned through past performance. Democratic leadership can lead to higher morale and productivity with those you lead. Authors Tom Peters and Nancy Austin recorded these observations about productivity: "The number one managerial productivity problem in America is, quite simply, managers who are out of touch with their people and out of touch with their customers."[8] However, democratic leadership is not without challenges. This leadership style can often lead to miscommunication and ambiguity in understanding one's role within the virtual community. Democratic leadership requires a time commitment, which can be difficult in a virtual work environment because time is typically the one variable there is never enough of. So which style of leadership is most effective in a virtual work environment?

The answer may surprise you: both. Allow the data to determine how you customize your leadership approach. For those individuals who are consistently engaging and are at or ahead of pace, a democratic or participative approach may make sense. However, for those individuals who are not consistently engaging or are behind pace, I would encourage you to employ a combination of both autocratic leadership

---

8. Tom Peters and Nancy Austin, quoted in Donald Walton, *Are You Communicating? You Can't Manage Without It.* (McGraw-Hill, 1991), 48.

and democratic leadership. The key is balance. Too much sugar, and the outcome will be apathy and the equivalent of managerial enabling. Too much spice, and the result will be a bitter employee who may sabotage your team and ultimately leave the organization. What you are after here is equity, or a healthy tension between the two styles.

On the leadership continuum, a horizontal line represents a continuous sequence in which adjacent elements are not distinctly different from one another, although the extremes are unmistakable. The left side of the leadership continuum is a purely democratic leader. As you begin to slide toward the center, placement on the continuum indicates a leader fluent in both leadership styles and capable of employing both democratic and autocratic tendencies. The far-right side of the leadership continuum is a purely autocratic leader. So, where do you fall on the leadership continuum? Virtual leaders of the twenty-first century can slide across the spectrum based on the situational needs of the organization.

The Leadership Continuum

Democratic   Autocratic

The leadership continuum is also consistent with the coaching continuum. In practice situations and the locker room, coaches and their temperaments can range from positive to negative. Coaches are masters of motivation. Some of the best speeches I have ever heard in my life came from coaches who simply tell it like it is. Their words of wisdom and candid conversations are commonalities that all great coaches employ to maximize the individual potential of those they lead. In my opinion, the organizations of the future will be led by master communicators. Their ability to move the masses through the power of well-crafted words will be the number one soft skill that will be sought by twenty-first-century organizations worldwide.

CHAPTER 6

Virtual Work Communities

The role of a creative leader is not to have all the ideas; it's to create a culture where everyone can have ideas and feel that they're valued.

—Ken Robinson

hat is your organization's culture? Is it exclusive and segregated, or is it inclusive and full of trust? Trust is the glue that binds individuals to a cause greater than themselves. Trust is an individual choice that can be impacted by the culture of an organization. Trust is the foundation of effective communication, and neuroscience demonstrates that when individuals feel safe and valued, their brain releases a hormone called oxytocin into the bloodstream. When released, oxytocin creates confidence that leads individuals into a more collaborative state of mind.

Collaboration creates momentum, and momentum produces leverage. Leverage is the transmitting force that generates a virtual mechanical advantage. Success in the twenty-first-century economy means maximizing opportunities and virtual mechanical advantages over an extended period. There are no shortcuts to becoming a great virtual leader. Success does not come cheap.

The velocity of innovation in the twenty-first century necessarily reduces the amount of strategic planning an organization can undertake. Trust cultivated over time results in relationships being formed, and these relationships allow organizations to respond to spontaneous opportunities with speed and skill. Time is finite, so organizational agility and the ability to seize the moment separate the good from the great.

Therefore, virtual leaders must cultivate a culture of synergy, which Stephen R. Covey defined this way:

> Synergy is what happens when one plus one equals ten or a hundred or even a thousand! It's the profound result when two or more respectful human beings determine to go beyond their preconceived ideas to meet a great challenge.[1]

I graduated from high school in Shawnee, Oklahoma. We were known as the Shawnee Wolves, and one of the best examples I know of synergy is the wolfpack, which is a socially organized group that lives and hunts in packs. By working cooperatively with one another, the wolfpack can compete for food with other animals that are much bigger and stronger than they are. The synergy of the wolfpack is analogous to the cohesiveness of a high-functioning team, which maintains a group commitment to the individuals within your "wolfpack" and the tasks at hand. Virtual leaders have a high level of emotional intelligence (EQ) and strive to maintain a "we" not "me" attitude within the pack. As those you lead begin to assimilate into the group, pride begins to form, and unity soon follows.

---

1. Stephen R. Covey, quoted in Rob Elkington, *Exceptional Leadership by Design: How Design in Great Organizations Produces Great Leadership* (United Kingdom: Emerald Publishing Limited, 2018), 216.

Unity or integration creates a platform for virtual leaders to empower those they lead, and empowerment is the social currency of organizations in the twenty-first century. According to author Robert Adams, empowerment is:

> The capacity of individuals, groups and/or communities to take control of their circumstances, exercise power and achieve their own goals, and the process by which, individually and collectively, they are able to help themselves and others to maximize the quality of their lives.[2]

Creating a culture of empowerment has several advantages, as it:
- Models trust and confidence in those you lead
- Creates scalability in organizations experiencing rapid growth
- Improves staff morale and job satisfaction
- Creates a stronger commitment to the leadership and organization
- Increases the level of creativity and innovative thinking

The competitive landscape has expanded and changed the traditional hierarchical modus operandi. Advancements in technology have flattened the world around us, resulting in a 24/7 fast-paced economy that is both elusive and erratic. Organizations that are fat and bureaucratic will struggle with their centrist approach in the volatility of the future economy. You may be asking: How do I prevent my organization from becoming morbidly obese? In a word, *decentralization*. Decentralization is the tonic for bloated bureaucracies; it is the process by which the functions and powers of an organization, especially those pertaining to planning and decision-making, are redistributed or delegated away from a centralized approach to management.

---

2. Robert Adams, quoted in Barbra Teater, *An Introduction to Applying Social Work Theories and Methods* (United Kingdom: McGraw-Hill Education, 2014), 57.

Decentralization allows organizations of the future to delegate and disseminate functions related to performance. Outcomes often referred to as results become the standard of success in a decentralized virtual environment. Author Peter Drucker was one of the first to popularize the phrase "management by objectives" or "management by results"[3] when he published his theories in 1954. Management by objectives is the process of defining specific objectives that you can convey to those you lead and then deciding the sequence in which you and your direct reports will achieve those objectives.

Remember, what gets measured gets done. Quantifiable targets that measure performance create objective data points with which to discern progress. In a virtual work community, monitoring progress is critical to achieving goals and objectives. The focus on summative data creates a ubiquitous work environment in which geography becomes irrelevant.

Tearing down the traditional four walls allows organizations to focus their human resource efforts on talent, training, and evaluating performance. One benefit of focusing on quantifiable indicators is that employee evaluations can be simplified as they become less subjective. The result is a comprehensive and balanced evaluation system that should be inclusive of both objective and subjective data.

Virtual work communities are focused on training and retaining their best and brightest employees. Content should be reviewed annually to ensure that organizations are keeping up with the change of pace. The goal is to get sticky with the material used for training purposes by including audio, visual, and kinesthetic components that encompass a multitude of learning styles. Training and development should be designed and aligned to organizational needs, both present and future. Remember, the future will be full of ambiguity. Virtual work communities are full of adaptable leaders

---

3. Peter F. Drucker, *The Practice of Management* (The Netherlands: Taylor & Francis, 2012).

who understand uncertainty and embrace change. The Center for Creative Leadership states that adaptable people show three kinds of flexibility:

- Cognitive flexibility – The ability to use different thinking strategies and mental frameworks.
- Emotional flexibility – The ability to vary one's approach to dealing with the emotions of others.
- Dispositional flexibility – The ability to remain optimistic and, at the same time, realistic.

In addition to having adaptable leaders, virtual work communities must allow personalized digital learning to drive the training of employees in the twenty-first century. Skill development will be available in a variety of learning styles, allowing the consumer to learn 24/7 in their preferred modality and at their preferred pace.

Organizational attrition or churn is the nemesis of virtual work communities. Retirement is understandable, but there are times when resignations can be avoided. Organizations with a negative or toxic virtual work community have a higher churn rate. If your organization's annual turnover rate exceeds 20%, this certainly warrants discussion among senior administrators to fully comprehend the culture and virtual work community you are creating.

Virtual leadership begins with hiring individuals who demonstrate resilience or grit. The twenty-first-century economy is an enigma full of ups and downs. Assembling a team that has the wherewithal and willingness to stretch and be stretched creates a counterbalance to the volatile cycle to come. Leaders should be looking for prospective employees who embody critical soft skills or attributes that let them function as:

- Connectors – Individuals that have the innate ability to create a connection.
- Communicators – The ability to convey organizational tasks and objectives and the capacity to inspire and motivate others.

- Integrity – A firm commitment to morals and values creates assurance that individuals will be able to succeed in a virtual work environment full of ambiguity.
- Positive – Unyielding enthusiasm is infectious and creates a climate of affirmation.
- Mentors – Growing others is one of the highest callings of virtual leadership and essential in a rapid growth work environment.

CHAPTER 7

Servant Leadership

Your rewards in life will be in direct proportion to the value of your service to others.

—Brian Tracy

Successful virtual work communities are full of humble leaders. Humility and sacrifice are cornerstones and represent a shift in the mindset from focusing on ambition to focusing on serving others. The phrase *servant leadership* was popularized by Robert K. Greenleaf in his 1970 essay, "The Servant as Leader."[1] Servant leadership creates a bottom-up approach, a shift from the twentieth-century top-down, power pyramid approach to management. Based on the value of benevolence, servant leaders demonstrate several characteristics, including these traits outlined by Larry Spears:[2]

1. Empathy – Servant leaders have understanding and sensitivity to the feelings and emotions of those they lead.

---

1. Robert K. Greenleaf, *The Power of Servant-Leadership*, ed. Larry C. Spears (San Francisco: Berrett-Koehler, 1998).
2. Larry C. Spears, "Character and Servant Leadership: Ten Characteristics of Effective and Caring Leaders," *The Journal of Virtues & Leadership* 1, no. 1 (2010): 25–30, https://www.regent.edu/acad/global/publications/jvl/vol1_iss1/Spears_Final.pdf.

2. Listening – Servant leaders are active listeners that couple skill-ful questioning to create a constructive forum and dialogue for discussion.

3. Healing – Servant leaders understand the social and emotional needs of those they lead and work to make them whole again.

4. Awareness – Servant leaders awaken the emotional intelligence of those they lead.

5. Persuasion – Servant leaders unite those they lead and use persuasion rather than position to achieve organizational goals and objectives.

6. Conceptualization – Servant leaders create a vision that inspires those they lead to maximize their potential.

7. Foresight – Servant leaders utilize the lessons learned from their past to anticipate future outcomes.

8. Stewardship – Servant leaders are cultivators of trust and believe in service over self.

9. Commitment to the growth of people – Servant leaders are multipliers and genuinely committed to the growth and development of those they lead.

10. Building community – Servant leaders identify commonalities among those they lead and build consensus toward a common vision.

Servant leadership requires sacrifice. One of my favorite quotes of all time comes from author and motivational speaker Jim Rohn who said that "you are the average of the five people you spend the most time with."[3] Who are you spending your time with? The company you keep influences who you become because relationships are symbiotic and help to shape your character. Character casts a shadow that reflects your reputation. American businessman Warren Buffett had this to say about

---

3. Jim Rohn, quoted in Joe Sweeny and Mike Yorkey, *Moving the Needle: Get Clear, Get Free, and Get Going in Your Career, Business, and Life!* (Germany: Wiley, 2014), 137.

a person's reputation: "It takes 20 years to build a reputation and five minutes to ruin it. If you think about that you'll do things differently."[4]

The path to influence is paved with mentors who have had a willingness to listen. I am so thankful for the mentors I have had throughout my life. One mentor in particular who sticks out is former US Congressman J. C. Watts. I first met J. C. when I coached basketball at Eufaula High School. J. C. had graduated from Eufaula High School before becoming a Sooner, quarterbacking for the University of Oklahoma's football team. J. C. went on to play professional football in Canada in the CFL before becoming a US congressman. J. C. is active as a lobbyist in Washington, DC, and he is a renowned public speaker who travels the country speaking on various topics, including leadership. Despite all his commitments, J. C. still found opportunities to have one-on-one conversations with me when I was serving as the superintendent of Stidham Public Schools. Our conversations about family, faith, and my professional future took place at a pivotal time when I was grappling with some life-changing decisions. J. C.'s words of encouragement and wisdom and the confidence with which he spoke brought peace amid a personal storm. I will forever be grateful for the role that my friend and mentor, J. C. Watts, played during that pivotal time in my life.

The Bible says that we will reap what we sow. We all want to reap a great harvest, yet very few leaders are willing to take the time to mentor the next generation and *pay it forward*. *Merriam-Webster* defines *harvest* as "the quantity of a natural product gathered in a single season." Remember that the fewer the seeds you sow, the smaller the harvest for you and those you lead; appropriately, novelist Robert Louis Stevenson advised, "Don't judge each day by the harvest you reap, but by the seeds you plant."[5]

---

4. Warren Buffet, quoted in Steve Giles, *The Business Ethics Twin-Track: Combining Controls and Culture to Minimise Reputational Risk* (United Kingdom: Wiley, 2015), 97.
5. Robert Louis Stevenson, quoted in Stuart G. Walesh, *Engineering Your Future: The Professional Practice of Engineering* (Germany: Wiley, 2012), 33.

Mentoring others is an essential component of becoming a strong virtual leader. Successful mentors do not see individuals as they are; they see them as they could be. The remote work environment of the twenty-first century can be fraught with feelings of insecurity and isolation. If these emotions are not addressed, the individuals you lead can become detached, disconnected, and disengaged. Virtual leaders are connectors and encouragers who have a high level of emotional intelligence (EQ). George M. Adams referred to encouragement as "oxygen to the soul."[6]

Virtual leaders have a willingness to develop both the personal and professional character of those they lead. Mentors invest time to identify the goals and aspirations of those they are mentoring. Most employees have a desire for upward mobility but lack the necessary knowledge or experience to move up within their organization during the early stages of their careers. Mentors help bridge the gap by providing perspective and context by listening and occasionally offering advice. Organizations experiencing rapid growth are intentional about creating and sustaining mentor-mentee relationships during the initial employee orientation to attract and retain talent.

Digital disruption at the turn of the twenty-first century fed a start-up boom, and organizations across the globe are continuing to grow at warp speed, creating a whirlwind of rapid growth. A rapid growth work environment can be full of energy and excitement, but the challenges it presents can be just as daunting. If your organization is growing at a rate of 30% annually, you are what I would consider a rapid growth organization. Organizational resources can be spread thin during periods of rapid growth, creating a conundrum of controlled chaos for virtual leaders who are being asked to increase productivity and simultaneously decrease instability.

Hiring and onboarding new employees in a rapid growth environment can also be challenging as human resource departments are

---

6. George M. Adams, quoted in John C. Maxwell and Jim Dornan, *How to Influence People: Make a Difference in Your World* (Nashville, TN: Thomas Nelson, 2013), 30.

pushed to the brink to supply the ever-growing demand for quality applicants. If you're not careful, quantity can take precedence over quality in the name of expediency, leaving in its wake a subset of new employees not equipped to perform their job functions. Training places additional pressure on processes and procedures as organizations work at a frenzied pace to develop their newest assets. Promotions of young and inexperienced leaders can pose problems over time as the blind begin leading the blind. Conflict is inevitable in a rapid growth environment leaving leaders within the organization feeling like firefighters as they tame the fearless flames known as rapid growth. The simple solution to solve the rapid growth equation is multiplication.

Multiplication increases the supply or surplus of potential employees by proactively prospecting individuals who demonstrate the propensity to lead and influence others. Multipliers are inclusive and focused on integration. Multiplication requires a shift in mindset from focusing exclusively on performance to focusing on individual employees as well. Human beings rarely depreciate but do require a consistent deposit or investment of time. Remember, time is a variable that is in high demand but short supply in a virtual work community. Virtual leaders manipulate time by delegating assignments and allocating authority to create capacity for the development of others.

The development of others in your organization is one of the highest callings of virtual leadership. Leaders who are self-centered or insecure in their leadership will struggle with this calling. The Bible reminds us to be quick to hear and slow to speak. During the mentoring of others, it is far better to lead through questions rather than answers. Questions create curiosity, which is the genesis of all knowledge. Questions are contagious and open the door to a higher cognitive state where the individual you mentor can begin to absorb the lessons learned and fit the pieces of the puzzle together on their time.

Virtual work communities cannot sustain success without creating a culture of coaching and mentoring. Virtual leaders should be scouring their virtual work communities to identify up-and-comers who have a positive attitude, are action-oriented, and have demonstrated a quantifiable ability to produce over time. These individuals have been forged by the fires of adversity and will bring a unique perspective that only experience can teach. Prospects for mentoring should demonstrate the following characteristics:

- A willingness and desire to receive additional assignments.
- A problem-solving mindset with the ability to creatively think outside the box to identify and implement solutions.
- A willingness to receive constructive coaching well and acknowledge areas of improvement.
- A collaborative and inclusive attitude that demonstrates respect for alternative viewpoints.
- A commitment to mentoring others and multiplying themselves.

Twenty-first-century organizations should focus on constructing a virtual work community for their constituents—communities that create compassion, which allows commonalities and relationships to be revealed among members. Relationships build influence. Influence produces impact. Impact is the invisible force that embodies a healthy culture and allows progress to be sustained over time. Sustained progress, not perfection, is the best indicator of a high-performance culture in the twenty-first century.

As we have worked our way through the first seven chapters of this book, you are well on your way to maximizing your leadership and influence with others. In the coming chapters, we will turn our attention away from the organization and resume our focus on your health and wellness as a leader and on those you lead. So, let's turn the page and open up Chapter 8 to begin that shift.

CHAPTER 8

Health and Wellness

The first wealth is health.

—Ralph Waldo Emerson

The world we live in has a variety of problems, but one of the chief culprits is an aversion to being average. Society has perpetuated the myth that average is not good by creating an unrealistic standard or ideal by which people can consistently measure themselves. The rise of social media and the 24/7 connectivity we share are daily reminders of how we are or are not measuring up. Upward mobility and an obsession with the proverbial climb have left in their wake a generation of overworked and underpaid individuals who are dissatisfied with their current reality. The mitigating effects of physical boundaries have also become blurred.

The traditional 40-hour workweek has been replaced with a new standard 60-hour workweek. The time-honored commute has been hijacked with online meetings and hands-free phone calls courtesy of Bluetooth technology. Cherished time at home with family and friends in what used to be known as after-hours has been disrupted by the constant contact of our smart devices. The pursuit of perfection has individuals sacrificing both their health and wellness in the name of middle-class warfare. Continual neglect eventually takes its toll, leaving individuals vulnerable to stress, anxiety, and even depression. Burn-out is real.

Johann Wolfgang von Goethe said, "It is not doing the thing we like to do, but liking the thing we have to do, that makes life blessed."[1] Over time, stress develops into fatigue. A by-product of fatigue is inactivity, which, in turn, affects the amount of energy your body will produce, leading to lethargy. Over time, lethargy can lead to a loss of willpower, and a host of health problems, such as cardiovascular disease, a weakened immune system, and reduced cognitive functioning, can arise. Individuals under continual stress tend to reach for coping mechanisms such as alcohol, smoking, food, and even prescription drugs—mechanisms that can create an unhealthy imbalance in one's body chemistry.

Understanding Work-Life Balance

Organizations of the twenty-first century are beginning to look in the mirror and take notice, and as a result, work-life balance is becoming a core component of their culture. Virtual leaders understand the vital role physical health plays in the work environment and that prioritizing the health and well-being of individuals you lead can reduce stress and lead to greater job satisfaction. Here are five examples of daily activities that you and those you lead can do to maintain a healthy work-life balance:

1. Going to bed earlier – Getting seven to eight hours of sleep per night is essential for most adults to function at a level of peak performance.

2. Exercise – People who do regular activity have a lower risk of many chronic diseases, such as heart disease, type 2 diabetes, stroke, and some cancers.

---

1. Johann Wolfgang von Goethe, quoted in Jan Malloch, *The Positive Achiever—11 Essentials to Achieve the Success You Deserve* (Lulu Enterprises Incorporated, 2009), 88.

3. Eat healthier foods – Preparing a few healthy snacks will help fight hunger and help you maintain a healthy weight.
4. Read – One 2009 study showed that reading may reduce stress by as much as 68%.
5. Meditate or pray – Gratefulness for life's blessings creates internal peace.

Eight Essentials of Wellness

The eight essentials of wellness are a great place to start a discussion about the health and wellness of each individual in your organization. Virtual leadership is about creating the conditions that are conducive to holistic wellness. By embracing the personal health and well-being of those you lead, you are sending a message that you care about more than just the bottom line. Through modeling

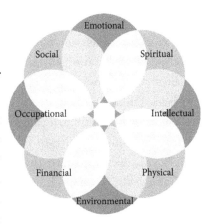

Wellness

and mentoring, virtual leaders can encourage healthy behaviors and support those they lead. I have found throughout my professional career that people typically do what they observe.

Emotional well-being is an essential component of every leader's health and wellness; therefore, leaders in the twenty-first century should strive for an emotional equilibrium. American writer and lecturer Dale Carnegie observed that "happiness doesn't depend on any external conditions, it is governed by our mental attitude."[2] Your attitude will dictate your actions, so creating emotional harmony in the form of

---

2. Dale Carnegie, quoted in Mathew Hartley, *One Month to Happiness* (United Kingdom: Lulu.com, 2011), 69.

balance ensures an equitable energy flow. Balance will build a personal bridge from emotional exposure to one of safety and shelter.

Emotional safety and stability create the conditions for relationships with those you lead to bloom. It has been said that relationships are forged, not formed and that initiating and sustaining relationships with those you lead is the best way to maintain emotional well-being through the ups and downs. Virtual leaders who can demonstrate healthy emotional wellness possess a natural authenticity and an attitude of gratitude. Remember, enthusiasm is contagious, and those you lead will begin to pattern their emotions through the professional conduit you construct within your organization's culture.

Preserving a positive and thankful attitude models grace for those you lead. Embracing both success and failure as teachable moments demonstrates humility. Arrogance is the fragrance of success, whereas failure is humbling. Strive to be confident but not prideful. Author John C. Maxwell explained that "there are two kinds of pride, both good and bad. 'Good pride' represents our dignity and self-respect. 'Bad pride' is the deadly sin of superiority that reeks of conceit and arrogance."[3] Progress cannot be achieved without taking risks, so embrace the prospect and possibility that you will experience setbacks and frustration along your journey, knowing that perseverance and wisdom will be your reward.

Individuals have an innate desire to connect; this human desire has evolved. Initially, our ancestors lived in caves and a state of isolation. However, they learned that there is security in numbers. As a result, social communities have formed over time. At first, these social communities were contingent on geography, made up of those living near one another and near resources, such as water, that they needed to survive. However, societies evolved as transportation became cheaper and more readily available, and by the turn of the twenty-first century,

---

3. John C. Maxwell, quoted in Kelly Lovell, *You'll Be Hearing from My Lawyer* (Lulu. com, 2016), 29.

a new technology was born as social media began to emerge. Social media spawned online communities and allowed individuals to connect regardless of their geography. Freedom of expression in the form of opinions and ideas proliferated around the globe providing a forum for anyone connected to the internet. This virtual gathering is available 24/7 for people who desire to connect with like-minded individuals.

Maximizing your leadership potential requires a commitment to connect with others. Networking can be done offline or online through the various social media platforms. I have to admit that connecting is one of my weaknesses as a leader. I am a natural introvert and, as such, I desire space and distance from others to recharge my batteries. However, I also understand I cannot effectively lead those with whom I do not have a relationship, so I am continually reminding myself to cultivate relationships and connections with coworkers. *Merriam-Webster* defines the term *cultivate* as: "to improve by labor, care, or study."

Virtual leaders develop cooperative virtual work communities that promote self-analysis and self-discovery. These virtual work communities are founded on shared beliefs and values that bind members of the community to a cause greater than themselves. As discussed in Chapter 6, relationships are formed and nurtured in these symbiotic communities. These relationships support and sustain the health and well-being of individuals in the virtual work community by creating a sense of belonging.

I want to ask you a question: Are you consistently growing and developing yourself as a leader? Intellectual stimulation is another necessary component to maintaining your overall health and wellness. Advancements and acceleration have torn down traditional barriers to acquiring knowledge. The World Wide Web and its infinite resources have created a global network where ideas can be discussed, debated, and disseminated.

Expanding your knowledge in the twenty-first century is no longer optional; it is an expectation if leaders are to keep up with an evolving economy. Like a woodsman who sharpens his ax before searching for firewood, individuals must continually hone their skill set and creative abilities through learning opportunities. Author and humorist Mark Twain quipped, "A person who won't read has no advantage over one who can't read."[4] Some of my favorite examples of growth and development opportunities include audiobooks, online courses, and TED Talks.

Did you know the company you keep also has an impact on your overall health and wellness? Virtual leaders understand the value of association and seek social solidarity. Positive, nurturing virtual communities foster a foundation that can mitigate worry and stress. Constructing a cocoon of stimulation and support will allow you to maintain an equilibrium of balance.

Maintaining emotional equilibrium in the twenty-first century requires you to disconnect so you can reconnect. Did you catch that? Solitude and silence are good for your soul. Being intentional about creating time to retreat and restore your mind will allow you to tap into your inner sense of purpose and meaning in life. Unless I am dealing with a crisis at work during the evening hours, you will find me unplugged from the responsibilities of work and mentally recharging with my wife and children. Among other things, we love to watch the Oklahoma City Thunder basketball team on television together. This time with my family rejuvenates me and renews my why.

Creating emotional clarity and calmness is essential to renewing harmony and maintaining a healthy balance. Does your workplace provide you with personal satisfaction and a sense of enrichment? Occupational optimism is another contributor to your overall health and wellness. Your thoughts have a direct impact on your attitude, which functions like a giant magnet attracting both positive and negative circumstances and individuals into your life. Consider this

---

4. Mark Twain, quoted in Pat Williams and Peggy Matthews Rose, *Read for Your Life: 11 Ways to Transform Your Life with Books* (Deerfield Beach, FL: Health Communications Inc, 2007), 4.

observation made by John C. Maxwell: "Who you are is who you attract. If you want to attract better people, become the kind of person you desire to attract."[5]

Virtual leaders derive satisfaction and fulfillment from their work. Work should be challenging and should consistently push you out of your comfort zone. Does your work stretch you? A monotonous work environment creates the conditions for apathy, complacency, and excuses to set in. Although life is full of adversity, the key is to learn from your losses by taking personal responsibility. You cannot maximize your potential or the potential of those you lead by pointing fingers and making excuses. Legendary UCLA basketball coach John Wooden said this about making excuses: "Never make excuses. Your friends don't need them and your foes won't believe them."[6]

Virtual leaders don't make excuses. They take responsibility, embrace opportunity, and follow through on the commitments they have made. Author Kenneth Blanchard says, "There's a difference between interest and commitment. When you're interested in doing something, you do it only when it is convenient. When you're committed to something, you accept no excuses, only results."[7] Virtual leaders work to create conditions that allow individuals to achieve peak performance. Setbacks and frustrations in the workplace are inevitable, and it takes real courage to persevere, overcome occupational adversity, and finish the race.

---

5. John C. Maxwell, quoted in Bobby Albert, *True North Business: A Leader's Guide to Extraordinary Growth and Impact* (New York: Morgan James Publishing, 2019), E-book.
6. John Wooden, quoted in Pat Williams and David Wimbish, *How to Be Like Coach Wooden: Life Lessons from Basketball's Greatest Leader* (Deerfield Beach, FL: Health Communications, Inc, 2006), 213.
7. Kenneth Blanchard, quoted in Wendy Weikal-Beauchat, *Courage for the Journey: Wisdom for the Broken Road* (Bloomington, IN: AuthorHouse, 2013), 19.

The last of the eight essentials impacting your overall health and wellness is your current financial situation. Are you content with your current fiscal reality and the potential for upward mobility within your organization? Financial stress is one of the leading causes of workplace dissatisfaction and the genesis of occupational attrition.

I want to be candid with you and tell you something that your boss might not be willing to share. Your compensation is in direct proportion to the value you bring to your organization. Did I step on your toes? I also tend to do that with the people I work with. There is good news, though. If you do not like your current compensation level, simply increase your value. Increase your skills, scope of influence, and performance, and most organizations will recognize your value to the organization's overall output and compensate you at a level commensurate with that value.

Don't be a complainer. Complainers perpetuate a victim mentality and a sense of entitlement. You are not a victim. You are better than that. If your current employer does not recognize your value over the long term, simply explore other employment opportunities. Nothing creates clarity for those in charge faster than having other organizations competing for your services. Your satisfaction with your current and future financial situation is essential to maintaining a positive attitude and sustaining your overall health and well-being.

I want to encourage you to close this book and take some time for reflection on your overall health and wellness. Are you currently moving in the right direction or wrong direction when it comes to the eight essentials of wellness? Here is a quick way to quantify your health and wellness.

- On a scale of 1 to 10, give yourself a score in all eight categories.
- Take your cumulative score and divide it by 8. The answer will provide you with a decimal point that you can convert into a percentage.
- Write that percentage down and put a reminder on your calendar to recalculate every three months.

This one calculation will create a consistent measurement for you through the various seasons of your life and will generate a gauge by which you can assess your overall health and wellness.

Leading a healthier lifestyle has multiple advantages for you and those you lead. Focusing on your body's health and wellness will reduce stress and anxiety. Prioritizing your health and well-being will also boost your attitude, which will increase the overall morale of your team. By developing healthy habits, your absenteeism rate will decrease, and departmental productivity will increase. A healthy body equals a healthy mind, and a healthy mind equals maximum performance.

CHAPTER 9

Experiential Learning

In the past a leader was a boss. Today's leaders must be partners with their people; they no longer can lead solely based on positional power.

—Ken Blanchard

As I write this book, I have spent the past 44 years surrounded by some of the best coaches this great country has to offer. From collegiate to high school varsity sports and from the early stages of middle school to the national AAU circuit, I have had the privilege of meeting and discussing leadership strategy with some of the best minds in athletics. I can tell you without hesitation that there is an art to coaching the people you lead. I was born to be a coach.

My journey began in the desert town of Yuma, Arizona, on the border of Mexico. My father was coaching collegiate men's basketball at Arizona Western Junior College. When I was born, rumor had it that I had a basketball in my crib before I left the hospital. Coaching is a mobile profession, much like preaching. So, after a couple of years, my father left AWJC to return to his alma mater, Oklahoma Baptist University, located in Shawnee, Oklahoma.

My earliest recollections of childhood are filled with memories of attending practice with my father in Clark Craig Fieldhouse on the campus of Oklahoma Baptist University. It was a different time then; my brothers and I were given free access to explore independently. Occasionally, the whistle would blow, and the ball would stop bouncing, and I would hear my father impart words of wisdom to his basketball team. Sometimes, the insight would be like a father talking to his son, but more often, it would be in the form of a much louder whole-group discussion.

As I said, coaching runs in my family. My father played for and worked as a graduate assistant under the direction of legendary college basketball coach Eddie Sutton. Coach Sutton was recently inducted into the Naismith Memorial Basketball Hall of Fame. He was a four-time National Coach of the Year winner who accumulated 806 wins as a head coach in college basketball. My older brother, Scott, was a coach, and I coached before getting into education administration. My younger brother, Mike, is a successful high school coach in the state of Oklahoma. Ironically, both of my sons, Bo and Jake, desire to become basketball coaches when they complete their college studies. You could say that coaching is in our DNA.

I believe virtual leaders must also be coaches. I would define coaching as the sequential unlocking of the mind to raise awareness and maximize individual potential toward the achievement of a team goal. Virtual leadership involves sharpening the skills of those you lead through experiential learning opportunities and inquiry. Experiential learning is foundational to virtual leadership and can provide up to 70% of a person's understanding. The 70/20/10 rules for leadership development created by the Center for Creative Leadership show how executives learn:

- 70% of their learning occurred through on-the-job experiences and challenges.
- 20% of their learning occurred from other people, such as a coach or mentor.

- 10% of their learning came from training courses or formal instruction.[1]

The search for answers always begins with a question because questions arouse the imagination and inspire innovation. Inquiry is becoming a scarce commodity in the twenty-first century. So many of today's start-up companies are founded by brilliant entrepreneurs who are leveraging the economic renaissance provided through digital technology. However, the youthful passion and tireless work ethic that it takes to start a business can mean that the leaders lack the leadership experience, context, and perspective necessary to sustain a thriving business. Production and performance quickly replace inquiry, a choice that will eventually lead down a dead-end road.

Young companies staffed with immature leaders tend to misperceive inquiry as an indictment of the organization. The fact that competence and execution supplant consistent questioning should come as no surprise. In my profession, traditional public schools have been preparing students for the factory for well over a century. Have you ever noticed that as students progress through school, they typically ask fewer questions? Yet we know that the concepts and curriculum become more advanced as students get older. So why do students ask fewer questions? The disintegration of inquiry can be found in the framework and structure of many public schools today.

After the industrial revolution, most modern nations saw the need to produce laborers for the factory. Concepts such as independent thinking were unnecessary. Obedience, compliance, and conformity were the preferred attributes of the factory workers in the nineteenth and twentieth centuries. Consequently, most public schools acquiesced to the demands of the economy of the day and lost sight of their fundamental

---

1. Douglas D. Riddle, Emily R. Hoole, and Elizabeth C. D. Gullette, *Center for Creative Leadership Handbook of Coaching in Organizations* (San Francisco: John Wiley & Sons, 2015).

pedagogy and purpose. This capitulation can still be found in many public schools today, particularly in inner-city urban schools attended by students who come from a lower socioeconomic background. Drop-out rates in certain urban high school districts can be as high as 50% (one out of every two students). This statistic is unacceptable.

In today's economy of rapid change, twenty-first-century organizations must confront the unpredictability of the future by going back to the basics of childhood and experiential learning. Curiosity that questions the status quo paves the way for twenty-first-century organizations to remain relevant and on the cutting edge.

Most corporations of the twentieth century were built with a standardized structure in which layers of bureaucracy created an invisible line of demarcation between the haves and the have nots. Questions from workers were typically suppressed by leadership because they feared that questions would expose their lack of knowledge and undermine their credibility. Vulnerability was perceived as a sign of weakness. How times have changed.

I currently lead a school district that employs thousands of individuals, and I can tell you unequivocally that I value vulnerability in those I lead. Virtual leaders embrace vulnerability as an opportunity to demonstrate maturity. One lesson I have learned in my years of virtual leadership is that today's solutions may not answer tomorrow's questions. Virtual leaders must adapt and evolve at the economy's rate of change. Competence has a shorter shelf life than ever before.

Inquiry sells and scales. Fostering a culture of investigation can be a catalyst for change. Inquiry can come in multiple forms, but my preferred method has its roots in the form of Socratic questioning to create a deeper, more meaningful conversation that cultivates creativity through exploration—what I refer to as plowing. *Merriam-Webster* defines *plowing* as: "to cut into, open, or make furrows or ridges." Plowing allows a farmer to plant the seed safely into the ground so it can grow and develop unimpeded. The wind may blow, and the storms may come, but the seed will sit safely planted until it is ready to germinate.

Virtual leaders prioritize the asking of penetrating questions over merely disbursing advice to those they lead. Socratic questioning intentionally slows the teaching and learning process down to a methodical pace. Questions connect virtual leaders to those they lead and offer a forum for growth and self-development. Another valuable lesson I have learned during my professional journey is that sometimes the hardest person to lead is yourself. The reason for this is that we all have blind spots that are difficult to detect without the help of others. As individuals, we tend to judge ourselves by our thoughts, yet we judge others by their actions.

Socratic questioning is open-ended, allowing for a broad exploration of blind spots and biases. Socratic questioning takes place in a safe zone where participants feel protected to question their common assumptions without fear of embarrassment or retribution. Virtual leaders work to create an inclusive culture where diversity is valued, and alternative viewpoints are respected. Tolerance is essential and ultimately will lead to a broader perspective on multiple topics that will break down barriers, allowing for collaboration, teaching, and experiential learning to take place.

Experiential learning is cyclical and can occur at regular intervals through a process known as the cycle of inquiry, which allows virtual leaders to focus on results for continuous experiential learning that leads to organizational improvement. The cycle of inquiry consists of the following five steps:

1. Setting SMART goals
2. Planning
3. Taking action
4. Assessing
5. Reflecting and adjusting

The first step virtual leaders take with those they lead through the cycle of inquiry is setting SMART goals. Remember from Chapter 4, SMART goals are specific, measurable, attainable, relevant, and timely.

Goals can be set in three forms. The first type of goal is an organizational goal; the second type of goal is a departmental goal. And the third type of goal is a personal or individual goal. What is it you hope to achieve? Defining the goal takes the abstract and makes it concrete. Writing your goals down creates an additional layer of accountability. Finally, sharing your SMART goals with your direct supervisor will allow that person to hold you accountable to the goals you have created.

The second step in the cycle of inquiry is planning. Now that you have defined your goals and the results you hope to attain, how will you get there? In coaching terms, what is the game plan? Virtual leaders simplify the complex by drawing on their own experience and breaking down the steps necessary to achieve success or victory. By analyzing historical data and key performance indicators consistently, patterns will begin to emerge. Planning is the strategy of overcoming the predictable patterns to make informed decisions that will lead to execution. *Merriam-Webster* defines *strategy* as "the art of devising or employing plans toward a goal."

The third step in the cycle of inquiry is taking action. The best plans in the world are meaningless if you don't take action. Action leads to discovery. Discovery is simply connecting new concepts that yield understanding; I call this connecting the dots. Understanding produces knowledge, and that leads to the fourth step in the cycle of inquiry.

The fourth step in the cycle of inquiry is assessing. How do you know whether your plan is working? By assessing or measuring, virtual leaders can discern whether the current course of action is bearing fruit or whether course corrections are needed to reach the final destination. Virtual leaders are responsible for navigating uncharted waters for those they lead. Assessing should be done at regular intervals to create a consistent pattern of accountability.

The fifth and final step in the cycle of inquiry is reflecting and adjusting. Be intentional about creating space and time for those you lead to reflect. Reflection is simply the review of the process and the outcomes or results of the assessment just performed. Space and time allow those you lead to process what just happened. Did we achieve our SMART goals? Virtual leaders should serve in the role of the county coroner and perform an autopsy or postmortem at each interval to dissect both the quantitative and qualitative data to raise awareness and inform future decision-making. Adjustments lead to congruence and conformity with the current external conditions. It is through the process of reflecting and adjusting that those you lead gain competence. Competence creates a context that informs the SMART goal setting process during the next cycle of inquiry.

The cycle of inquiry is intended to create a consistent loop of improvement or meaningful change that allows virtual leaders and organizations to keep up with the unpredictable pace and volatility of the twenty-first century. By creating a culture of inquiry that supports experimentation and risk-taking, virtual leaders reduce uncertainty by empowering those they lead to own their results and performance.

Great leaders define reality for those they lead, and virtual leaders strive to maintain a healthy balance between idealism and realism. American businessman and author Max Depree said that "the first responsibility of a leader is to define reality. The last is to say thank you. In between, the leader is a servant."[2] Realities come in a variety of forms, such as fiscal realities, personnel realities, and deadline realities.

The key to experiential learning is not to get bogged down in the swamp of responsibilities because the swamp simply slows ideas and innovation down to a slog. Pausing at regular intervals to take a step back, reassess, and to see whether an adjustment is needed differentiates between organizations that merely survive and those that thrive. Regular reflection and adjustments will give you a 360-degree perspective that allows you to gain your navigational bearings. I refer to these adjustments as pivoting.

---

2. Max Depree quoted in Eric J. Russell, *In Command of Guardians: Executive Servant Leadership for the Community of Responders* (Germany: Springer International Publishing, 2016), 61.

In the game of basketball, pivoting is stepping with one foot while keeping the other foot at its point of contact with the playing floor. A basketball player can turn in a 360-degree radius to gain clarity. Clarity is essential to operate effectively in the virtual work environment, which is more volatile and less predictable than its brick-and-mortar counterpart. The landscape will be full of jagged rocks and barriers along your virtual leadership climb. Pivoting is not only acceptable but necessary to be a proactive virtual leader.

Proactive virtual leaders anticipate problems, changes, or needs for those they lead. The challenge is that most organizations and, thus, most leaders are reactive in their response to change. Change is inevitable; the variable is the rate of change. Transformation is similar to playing defense in athletics. Defense typically comes in two varieties: zone or man to man. Man-to-man defense is reactive and primarily an individual response to what the person you are defending is doing, whereas a zone defense is more proactive and a team response to where the ball is located. Defenders are strategically placed in locations in anticipation of where the ball might be. Playing zone is typically more difficult because it is a structured approach that requires the coordination of the whole team to execute effectively. However, if the team can communicate synergistically, a zone defense can respond to rapid shifts in ball movement or, in business terms, the market economy.

Virtual leaders are committed to empowering those they lead through a process known as an apprenticeship, which is a form of experiential learning and empowerment that has been around for centuries. An apprenticeship could be defined as an arrangement between two individuals whereby the transfer of knowledge can occur.

Independent experiential learning is a messy process. Virtual leaders should strive to create a safe ecosystem with the freedom to fail. Failure is an opportunity disguised as a crisis. It is our response to the crisis or opportunity that defines us as leaders. I am reminded of the analogy of the duck swimming across the pond. On top of the water, the duck appears to be gliding gracefully across the water, but underneath the surface, the duck is paddling furiously to stay afloat. One way to create some intentional space for experiential learning and the inevitable failure is through contingency planning. I refer to contingency planning as Plan B. Interweaving Plan B contingencies into your nomenclature, coaching, and experiential learning gives the individuals you lead the confidence to fail forward.

Plan B sets the stage for pivoting. Pivoting establishes the expectation that if Plan A is not working, we are not going to continue to do the same thing and expect different results. Virtual leaders must set up routine evaluations of those they lead to discuss key performance indicators. Are we making progress? Yes or no? If the answer is yes, we continue with Plan A. If the answer is no, we pivot to Plan B. These evaluations or conversations should be occurring regularly to create a consistent feedback loop as part of the experiential learning process. John C. Maxwell offered this valuable clarification: "Failed plans should not be interpreted as a failed vision. Visions don't change, they are only refined. Plans rarely stay the same, and are scrapped or adjusted as needed. Be stubborn about the vision, but flexible with your plan."[3]

Have you ever wondered why learning occurs for some but not for others? The human brain comprises over 100 million neurons, yet it is still one of the least understood organs in the human body. In the next chapter, we will step into the human mind to explore learning and individual motivation.

---

3. John C. Maxwell, quoted in Jennifer LeClaire, *Dream Wild*, 164.

CHAPTER 10

Casting a Vision

Leadership is the capacity to translate vision into reality.

—Warren G. Bennis

The future belongs to the dreamers. Without them, we would still be driving around in horse-drawn buggies and living in houses without electricity or running water. The genesis of innovation begins with the imagination. Steve Jobs imagined a world where every home had a personal computer. Jeff Bezos envisioned a world where goods could be purchased from your smartphone and delivered to your door in just two days.

History is full of disruptors to the status quo. These individuals refused to accept the excuse that this is the way we have always done it. Instead, they have demonstrated a desire and willingness to think outside the box, to reimagine what could be; this innate need or desire is the secret sauce of creators. These artists of innovation create the music that you listen to and conceive the social media that you tend to. They are cultivators of the mind.

According to *Merriam-Webster*, the mind is the part of your body that "feels, perceives, thinks, wills, and especially reasons." What is beautiful about the human mind is that in most cases, it is under your control. Despite all the chaos and uncertainty in the world today, the management of your mind ultimately rests with you. You are what you think about almost all the time. Therefore, if you are willing to change your thoughts, you can change your life. I have seen this life-changing law work over and over in my life.

Unpredictability has become the new normal. Inevitably some of the individuals you lead will have an aversion to change. The aversion is a perfectly natural response to uncertainty brought on by homeostasis. In the study of biology, homeostasis is the state of regular or steady internal physical and chemical conditions maintained by living systems. This stasis or stagnation is generations in the making, and I commonly refer to it as the comfort zone. Have you ever tried to mold a hard piece of clay? Cognitive rigidity and inflexibility stem from familiarity and the brain's natural tendency to want to remain comfortable. Your body attempts to maintain a constant balance or equilibrium. Physiologically, this is necessary to maintain our body temperature and regulate other vital bodily functions. However, homeostasis can get in the way of embracing external change.

The harsh reality is that we live in a soft society filled with parents who have coddled their children. Gone are the days in youth sports when only the first-place team gets a trophy. Today, we pass out participation trophies like candy at Halloween and have cognitively confused the next generation. Folks, life is not always fair and equal. Life can be cold and cruel. The reality is we can only control what we can control; some things are simply out of our control. So, what do we control? We control how we prepare. Abraham Lincoln said: "Give me six hours to chop down a tree and I will spend the first four sharpening the axe."[1]

---

1. Abraham Lincoln, quoted in Akwasi O. Afriyie, *Pressing Forward: 7 Keys to Unleashing Your Full Potential!* (Author Solutions, 2014), 123.

Merriam-Webster defines *preparation* as "the action or process of getting ready for some occasion."

Virtual leaders must be prepared to confront comfort, complacency, and the status quo. American businessmen and author Farrah Gray said that "comfort is the enemy of achievement."[2] I often tell new employees I lead in their first year working in a remote work environment to get comfortable with being uncomfortable. Organizational foundations are typically constructed for stability and resistance to change. This resistance provides an infrastructure of consistency and cohesion. Policies and procedures are created to guide decision-making toward achieving rational outcomes. The irony is that the market in the twenty-first century is just the opposite; it is full of irrational and illogical volatility.

Disruption leads to destruction, and twenty-first-century organizations that fail to evolve will eventually die or be cast into a black hole of irrelevance. Let me give you two more historical examples recently cited in an article by David Capece:

> In an era that moved at a snail's pace compared to today, one Wall Street analyst wrote in 1910, "The world market for automobiles is at most 1 million units." His projection was based on the assumption that only 1 million families could afford chauffeurs. . . . In the late '90s, the world was abuzz with dot-com euphoria. In January 2000, the valuation of Yahoo! peaked at $140 billion. The theory was that the Internet was a transformative innovation, being adopted at warp speed. Nearly 15 years later, Yahoo!'s $28 billion valuation is dwarfed by Google's $290 billion valuation.[3]

---

2. Farrah Gray, quoted in Bill Jerome and Curtis Powell, *The Disposable Visionary: A Survival Guide for Change Agents* (ABC-CLIO, 2015), 75.
3. David Capece, "Adaptability: The Key to Leadership," *Wharton Magazine*, June 26, 2013, https://magazine.wharton.upenn.edu/digital/why-adaptability-is-the-key-ingredient-to-leadership-success/.

Disoriented employees who are struggling to keep up with the continual changes of the future have what I refer to as transitional fatigue. Organizations can tackle transitional fatigue by building change and innovation into their existing culture. Policies and procedures can be created and customized to recalibrate at fixed intervals. Modifications, also known as tweaks, create a biome of innovation whereby ideas can grow organically.

Innovation is iterative. Innovation, in most cases, is not one single idea but rather a culmination of smaller ideas coalesced into a congruent concept. English clergyman William Pollard said, "Learning and innovation go hand in hand. The arrogance of success is to think that what you did yesterday will be sufficient for tomorrow."[4] Virtual leaders are longitudinal thinkers. While most leaders are focused on the next one to three years, virtual leaders imagine a world five to 10 years from the present day.

As a brick-and-mortar superintendent, I can remember creating Oklahoma's first public school One-to-One initiative back in 2005. One-to-One simply means one laptop for every child. My administrative peers quickly criticized the move because of the cost and the fact that they had wired desktops in a computer lab setting. However, by putting mobile wireless laptops in the hands of every child, every day, I knew that we would have the opportunity to begin to personalize the learning experience for every child in our school. Children are unique, and although they may be the same age, they are typically at different learning levels. The investment we made in our One-to-One initiative increased learning opportunities and reduced discipline issues in the classroom. Fast-forward 15 years later, and you will find a significant number of schools throughout the United States employing One-to-One laptop initiatives with their student population.

---

4. C. William Pollard, *The Soul of the Firm* (Grand Rapids, MI: Zondervan, 1996), 107.

Innovation is also intuitive. English designer Jonathan Ive had this to say about innovation: "If you are truly innovating, you don't have a prototype you can refer to."[5] By consistently innovating and reframing your organization's challenges, your perception will produce new angles and new lenses with which to solve problems. One of the more popular phrases floating around twenty-first-century organizations is to "think outside the box." I have referred to the thinking outside the box multiple times already in this book. The box is simply a metaphor to represent the rigidity of our closed-minded thinking. Uncompromising thoughts limit our human beliefs, feelings, and creativity. By continually asking what is possible, virtual leaders expand beyond the crate of conventional wisdom. You may be asking yourself: How do I create the conditions and culture that promote outside the box thinking? Here are five of my favorite ways:

1. Provide those you lead the freedom to fail.
2. Create sustainable workloads that limit distractions.
3. Nurture those you lead by demonstrating confidence in their abilities.
4. Foster challenging work through cooperative goal setting that is rigorous but attainable.
5. Encourage collaboration by partnering with those you lead to tackle projects and challenges facing the organization.

Virtual leaders use a combination of cognition and intuition to shape decision-making in the twenty-first century. Awareness begins in the brain. Let's take a minute to have a science lesson on the brain. The brain is divided into two symmetrical cerebral hemispheres. The left part of our brain controls analytic thought, reasoning, and logic, and the right part of our brain coordinates creativity, imagination, and intuition. Awareness of the brain is key to understanding yourself and

---

5. Jonathan Ive, quoted in Kathleen R. Allen, *Launching New Ventures: An Entrepreneurial Approach* (Boston: Cengage Learning, 2015), 124.

those you lead. Advancements in technology and computer processing are allowing virtual leaders to utilize fewer left-brain functions and instead use more right-brain functions to create solutions to problems that do not even exist yet.

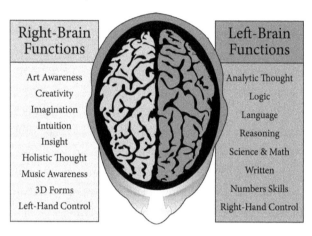

Right-Brain Functions	Left-Brain Functions
Art Awareness	Analytic Thought
Creativity	Logic
Imagination	Language
Intuition	Reasoning
Insight	Science & Math
Holistic Thought	Written
Music Awareness	Numbers Skills
3D Forms	Right-Hand Control
Left-Hand Control	

One of the right-brain activities is intuition. *Merriam-Webster* defines *intuition* as "the power or faculty of attaining to direct knowledge or cognition without evident rational thought and inference." An electromagnetic field of energy surrounds the world we live in. You can tap into this energy 24/7. In fact, you are already tapping into it on a nightly basis as you dream in your sleep. The loss of space and time as you dream is known as flow. This stream of unconsciousness aligns your mind and body with the universal flow of energy. If I told you I successfully predicted the gender of all three of my children through visions I had while sleeping, would you believe me?

Intuition allows you to peak into the future to create clarity by coordinating your personal and professional goals. Patterns create purpose by simplifying the complex. Remember, life in the twenty-first-century economy will be full of both change and ambiguity. Virtual leaders consistently use intuition to guide their judgment and decision-making, especially when data is minimal or nonexistent. Consider this statement commonly attributed to American humorist Will Rogers:

"Good judgment comes from experience, and a lot of that comes from bad judgment."

The ability to focus separates a mature virtual leader from an immature virtual leader. We live in a world of multitasking. Have you ever been driving down the highway and had the car in front of you unintentionally swerve into the median? You try to pass the individual and see they are text messaging on their smartphone while driving a vehicle at the speed limit. The prefrontal part of the brain is responsible for selective attention or what is sometimes referred to as focus.

Virtual leaders are masters of both self-awareness and self-control. Self-control is known as an executive function and is the restraint exercised over one's impulses, emotions, or desires. *Merriam-Webster* defines *self-awareness* as "an awareness of one's own personality or individuality."

The ability to subdue cognitive stimuli is essential in a world that is always powered on. Distractions are everywhere. Virtual leaders must be able to demonstrate mindfulness amid the storm. *Merriam-Webster* defines *mindfulness* as "the practice of maintaining a nonjudgmental state of heightened or complete awareness of one's thoughts, emotions, or experiences on a moment-to-moment basis." Mindfulness creates self-awareness, and self-awareness creates purpose.

Advancements in technology have allowed for just about every adult and teenager to walk around with a personal computer in their pocket. Although I am a proponent of technology and its use to improve our lives, there is an addictive quality to these tiny machines. Don't believe me? Next time you go to a large public gathering such as a basketball game, take a look at how many people are watching the game and how many are watching their phones, particularly during timeouts and in between quarters. This statement is particularly true for the next generation. My children's definition of adversity is hitting a dead spot while traveling in our car, where there is no Wi-Fi or cell phone reception for 30 minutes. They become agitated and upset when they are forced to engage in dialogue with one another for an extended period.

Do you find purpose in the work you do? Author and clergyman TD Jakes said it best: "If you can't figure out your purpose, figure out your passion. For your passion will lead you right into your purpose."[6] When you couple purpose with passion, you get significance. Significance is sustainable. Finding your purpose creates intrinsic motivation that will continue to fuel the fire of passion during the inevitable ups and downs of life.

Virtual leaders practice value-based leadership. Remember, we talked about values in Chapter 1. Values are the foundation of your beliefs, and they are nonnegotiable. Are your values in alignment with your thoughts and your actions? Author Brian Tracy says, "Just as your car runs more smoothly and requires less energy to go faster and farther when the wheels are in perfect alignment, you perform better when your thoughts, feelings, emotions, goals, and values are in balance."[7] Values give us something to lean on during times of uncertainty. They are a guiding light and set the standard of ethics one subscribes to. Value-based leaders inspire through example; they are role models in every sense. Virtual leaders practice value-based leadership and acknowledge these principles when they determine the prioritization of their goals.

On the opposite end of the spectrum are insecure leaders who manage by fear, intimidation, and control. They cultivate cultures of angst and anxiety, and they divide by promoting doubt and distrust of the very people they work with and the ideas they share. If you work in an oppressive or autocratic environment of suspicion, the best advice I can give you is to leave that organization. Companies that tolerate widespread authoritarian leadership are relics of the twentieth century and will die a slow and painful death in the future economy.

---

6. TD Jakes, quoted in Bruce Schultz, *The Passion Filled Life*, 59.
7. Brian Tracy, quoted in Marilyn Tam, *Living the Life of Your Dreams: The Secrets to Turning Your Dreams into Reality* (Cardiff, CA: Waterside Productions Inc, 2011), 13.

Virtual leaders are committed to engaging connected relationships. The keyword here is *engage*. Engage with the direct reports who make up your tribe; it is hard to influence someone with whom you do not have a relationship. Creating meaningful relationships takes time to understand both the individual and group dynamics. According to an article that Carolyn O'Hara published in the *Harvard Business Review*:

> Getting people to work together isn't easy, and unfortunately many leaders skip over the basics of team building in a rush to start achieving goals. But your actions in the first few weeks and months can have a major impact on whether your team ultimately delivers results.[8]

Communication builds relationships. Conversations begin with questions; spend some time getting to know your team individually by asking questions and listening intently. Ralph Nichols said, "The most basic of all human needs is the need to understand and be understood. The best way to understand people is to listen to them."[9] What do your direct reports need? Your direct reports want and need to connect. Remember, commonalities create connections, and connections that are fostered over time become the virtual glue that binds all high performing teams together.

The day was September 14, 1860. The circus had come to Ithaca, New York, and at first sight of the great Niagara Falls, a French tightrope walker named Charles Blondin stated that he believed he could become the first person to cross a tightrope stretched 1,100 feet across the falls. The distance was over a quarter of a mile connecting the United States to Canada. The height was 160 feet above the falls.

---

8. Carolyn O'Hara, "What New Team Leaders Should Do First," *Harvard Business Review*, (September 11, 2014), https://hbr.org/2014/09/what-new-team-leaders-should-do-first.
9. Ralph Nichols, quoted in A. B. Krizan, P. Merrier, K. S. Williams, and J. P. Logan, *Business Communication* (Boston: Cengage Learning, 2010), 461.

Blondin walked across the tightrope and began to systematically up the level of difficulty with each pass. Legend has it that Blondin crossed on stilts, in a sack, on a bicycle, in the dark, and even blindfolded. A large crowd gathered to watch Blondin defy death with each dangerous pass. After pushing a wheelbarrow holding a sack of potatoes across the tightrope, Blondin asked the audience: "Do you believe I can carry a person across in this wheelbarrow?" The crowd that had gathered passionately shouted: "Yes! We believe." "Okay," said Blondin, "get into the wheelbarrow." The crowd fell silent because this was the moment of truth.

Faith in the future is necessary, especially in an organization experiencing rapid growth. Creating a culture of authentic leadership and shared values will lay a solid foundation in the event your organization undergoes rapid growth. Scaling up is not uncommon in the twenty-first-century economy. Growth can be both a blessing and a curse. Have you heard of Packard's Law? It states that growth in revenues cannot exceed growth in people who can execute and sustain that growth. Rapid growth organizations can sow seeds of self-destruction if they fail to hire leaders who are authentic and have a growth mindset.

Author Carol Dweck is an expert on the topic of a growth mindset. She says that "most experts and great leaders agree that leaders are made, not born, and that they are made through their own drive for learning and self-improvement."[10] Leaders have either a fixed or a growth mindset. Leaders who believe that their personal qualities are fixed and unchangeable have a fixed mindset. Leaders who believe they can improve or change their personality traits over time have a growth mindset. As leaders get older, it is not uncommon to adopt more of a fixed mindset. Confidence acquired through experience blinds leaders to the priorities that originally led to their success.

Self-awareness is the only elixir to ego and pride. In the Bible, Proverbs 16:18 says: "Pride goes before destruction, a haughty spirit

---

10. Carol Dweck, "Warning Signs of an Unhealthy Appetite for Risk," *Harvard Business Review*, June 14, 2012, https://hbr.org/2012/06/how-a-fixed-mindset-feeds-an-u.

before a fall." Have you ever worked for a boss who takes the credit for all success and blames others for the failures of their department or organization? Don't be a narcissist. Mature virtual leaders consistently spread credit among the team and organization at large. John C. Maxwell urges leaders to keep these points in mind as they seek to build and maintain effective teams:

- The least important word: I
- The most important word: We
- The two most important words: Thank you.
- The three most important words: All is forgiven.
- The four most important words: What is your opinion?
- The five most important words: You did a good job.
- The six most important words: I want to understand you better.[11]

Self-awareness is another of the Top 10 soft skills that virtual leaders display. Now that we have a firm understanding of how our mind works and how to use various strategies for team building, let's discuss in detail the necessary ingredients to create a healthy work environment.

---

11. Maxwell and Dornan, *Becoming a Person of Influence.*

CHAPTER 11

Empathy and Accountability

Empathy is the starting point for creating a community and taking action. It's the impetus for creating change.

—Max Carver

One of the things I enjoy most about living in Oklahoma is the four seasons it produces on an annual basis. Because of its centralized location within the United States, it has a moderate climate. We experience summer, fall, winter, and spring seasons. Each of the four seasons has a beginning and an end. The virtual work environment of the twenty-first century is much the same way. There will be times of intense volume and endless hours that feel like they are never going to end. Yet, at times there are periods of relative tranquility when you can breathe and enjoy the freedom that can only come from working remotely.

The work environment of the future is built on the psychological Self-Determination Theory (SDT), which states that for those you lead to be happy in their work environment, they only need three things:

1. Autonomy – Self-directing freedom or control of how their time is managed.
2. Competence – Sufficient knowledge, judgment, or skill to perform their job.
3. Relatedness – A feeling of being connected to others and a higher cause.

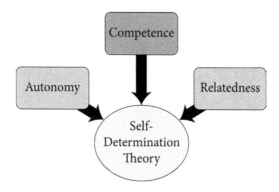

Attracting and retaining top talent requires a certain level of autonomy. Understand that in the virtual work environment, you are not competing with others as much as you are competing with yourself. How much of your capacity are you utilizing on a daily or weekly basis? Capacity can only be maximized and sustained through intrinsic motivation. Let me ask you two questions. First question: Do you like your job? Second question: Do you love your job? The distance between those two questions is where the feeling of trust resides. Employees want to feel their direct supervisor trusts them. Do you feel trusted to do your job? Do you have the independence and flexibility necessary to maximize your potential? Organizations that create cultures of autonomy while maintaining accountability will reap the rewards of employee satisfaction and longevity. This delicate balance is what separates a good organization from a great organization and ultimately will determine its failure or success.

Success is a by-product of checks and balances. The foundation of this healthy tension is the belief that we should trust but verify that those we lead are executing according to expectations. The phrase "trust but verify" was first made popular by former President of the United States Ronald Reagan during the Cold War era when referring to Mikhail Gorbachev and the Soviet Union. Virtual leaders understand that there are two possible reasons for the need to trust but verify. Perhaps those you are leading lack clarity due to the lens with which they are viewing your expectations. It was Earl Nightingale who said, "We tend to live up to our expectations."[1] Or perhaps your direct reports lack the necessary skills to perform their job function. When it comes to the fulfillment of tasks, you need to inspect what you expect.

There are two ways to supervise the completion of tasks. The first way is through abdication. *Merriam-Webster* defines *abdication* as "an act of abandoning or discarding a right, responsibility, etc." Abdication is indiscriminate and typical of naive first-generation leaders. Typically, abdication is done for the sake of expediency because of a perceived lack of time. Abdication simplified is: Trusting but not verifying. The second way to supervise the completion of tasks is through delegation. *Merriam-Webster* defines *delegation* as the ability to "entrust (a task or responsibility) to another." Delegation involves following up with integrity to ensure that the task assigned has been completed with fidelity. Former US Senator and US Congressman from North Dakota Byron Dorgan said, "You can delegate authority, but you cannot delegate responsibility."[2] Responsibility rests with you.

---

1. Earl Nightingale, quoted in Drew Laughlin, *Expect Success: How to Accomplish Anything in Life Using Your Inner Circle of Success* (Bloomington, IN: Black Shirt Publishing, 2009), 39.
2. Byron Dorgan, quoted in Jim Stroup, *Managing Leadership: Toward a New and Usable Understanding of What Leadership Really Is—and How to Manage It* (iUniverse, 2004), 59.

Employee satisfaction is also directly related to competence. Do your direct reports have the necessary skills, knowledge, and expertise to complete their job functions? If not, that's okay because competency can be developed through mentoring and training. There is a direct correlation between being proficient at your job and an increase in job satisfaction. When an employee understands what is expected of him or her, clarity develops, and a results-driven culture can be created. The final piece of the puzzle associated with the Self-Determination Theory (SDT) is relatedness.

Relatedness is a feeling of being connected to others and a higher cause. Time is finite. The workforce of the future does not want to waste time on missions and motives that lack purpose. Understanding the why is critical to gaining buy-in from your direct reports. Why does your organization need to exist? Organizations that lack purpose or relatedness simply become stagnant transactional institutions unable to grow and sustain their workforce with fidelity.

Why are so many employees dissatisfied with their current work environment? Some work environments are filled with fear. This twentieth-century mentality creates a culture of instability and perpetuates an us-against-them mentality. The concept of labor versus management dates back to the Industrial Revolution. Former President Abraham Lincoln said, "A house divided against itself cannot stand."[3]

Twenty-first-century organizations embrace diversity; they are inclusive work environments that value and seek employee feedback regularly. Creating the right conditions allows employees to maximize their potential and approach their work environment with confidence.

At the core of individual potential lies a foundation of fearlessness. The twenty-first-century work environment should be free from retribution and ridicule. Individuals are empowered to share their knowledge and ideas. Departments are set up as learning laboratories,

---

3. Abraham Lincoln, quoted in John Maxwell, *Beyond Talent: Become Someone Who Gets Extraordinary Results* (Nashville, TN: Thomas Nelson, 2011), 249.

and failure is embraced as part of the learning process. Growth and development are continuous. Does this sound like your organization? If not, your organization still has work to do. Psychological safety is essential to creating good work habits and trust.

Work environments that lack trust can be full of apathy and procrastination. Procrastination is simply a coping mechanism used by individuals with anxiety that prevents them from beginning or ending a task on time. This type of victim mentality is like cancer to the work environment. The cancer invades or spreads from person to person and eventually from department to department throughout the organization with indifference leaving a culture of lethargy in its wake.

Sometimes, lethargic behavior is due to feelings of being over-whelmed. Remember, tasks can typically be broken into smaller bite-sized chunks rather than trying to accomplish them all in one feeding. One of the best ways to break tasks down is to simplify. By simplifying down to the least common denominator, those you lead can gain confidence with each task that is completed. Remember, the goal is to create an independent and intrinsically motivated workforce that is capable of operating autonomously in your absence. If your direct reports are struggling to complete tasks on time, the first step is to take a long look in the mirror. What you see on the inside is a direct reflection of what they see on the outside. Clutter equals confusion. Encourage those you lead to prune their professional life by creating space. Maintaining a healthy work-life balance is essential to simplifying an employee's life and building good habits.

Producers get promoted. The topic of productivity is the holy grail of successful virtual leadership. Virtual leaders who produce are priceless to your organization and worth their weight in gold. These individuals are in high demand and short supply. It is through the consistent accomplishment of goals that leaders begin to differentiate themselves from their counterparts.

Success requires consistent execution at a high level. By creating an outcomes-based culture of performance within your organization, leaders ensure that their direct reports will remain focused on growth and achievement. At the end of the day, it is about results. Effective executives embrace the accountability associated with high expectations. By continuously focusing on improvement, virtual leaders foster efficiency and execution. Sustaining execution will require ongoing support.

Workplace nirvana includes both high challenge and high support. What is your culture's current level of sustenance? Conflict within a tribe is inevitable because the group is composed of individuals with differing motivations, values, and standards. As long as disagreement is respectful, it can lead to a healthy resolution. American politician Frank A. Clark said that "we find comfort among those who agree with us, and growth among those who don't."[4]

From children to spouses, finances to health, it is easy to lose focus on the daily work or cultivation that must be done to maintain a healthy culture. If you do not create a culture of consistent cultivation, then inevitably weeds will work their way into your tribe's soil. What damage will weeds do to your tribe's soil? Weeds compete for water, sunlight, and nutrients leaving non-weed plants starving. Because most weeds grow at such an astounding rate, they often absorb more of one nutrient than another, leaving an imbalance within the soil. Imbalance is a formula for failure.

Both empathy and accountability are crucial nutrients to a healthy work environment in the twenty-first century. Virtual leaders who build healthy cultures within their tribe will be able to bring both high challenge and high support at the appropriate time and place. By coupling accountability with technology and the tools of the future, virtual leaders can create the conditions that allow employees to not only survive but thrive.

---

4. Frank A. Clark, quoted in Ted Bagley, *My Personal War Within: "A Struggle to Find Inner Peace"* (United Kingdom: Xlibris, 2011), 163.

Let's step into the future in our final chapter together. I want to give you a glimpse of what you are going to see in the coming years and decades. The workforce of the future will look different for your children and grandchildren than what you currently see. Close your eyes, take a deep breath, turn the page, and let's step into the future together.

CHAPTER 12

Technology and the Future of Jobs

You cannot escape the responsibility of tomorrow by evading it today.

—Abraham Lincoln

There is no better example of economic disruption than the retail sector. Several retail businesses have been disrupted by improvements in technology during the last 10 years. Toys R Us, Blockbuster, Payless, Gymboree, and Borders have all closed their doors. Such digital restructuring is a foreshadowing of what is to come in the next decade. More corporations and their respective employees will fall victim to digital disruption. Let me give you a history lesson regarding other examples of digital disruption that have taken place since the dawn of time.

Once upon a time, ancient traditions were passed down from one generation to the next through oral storytelling that eventually gave way to the written word. Writings carved into rocks and mountains ultimately gave way to printing on papyrus. During the fifteenth century, the written word was multiplied through the Gutenberg printing press, allowing paper-based books to be printed and distributed in bulk throughout the world. The twentieth century saw an increase and an eventual decrease in the manufacturing and distribution of paper-based books. Paper-based books have given ground to digital e-book readers such as the Amazon Kindle or audiobooks through subscription-based apps like Audible. Consumers can now listen to their favorite book being read to them via their phone, tablet, or computer. E-books will also become obsolete in the future. The books of tomorrow will contain biometric sensors that read your body temperature, pulse, and other vital indicators allowing the plot in the story to change, including alternative endings based on your current mood.

Robots known as "bots" are already automating the performance of job duties in the auto industry, thereby decreasing the number of full-time employees an organization needs. Bots will take routine tasks and perform the job functions faster and more efficiently than their human counterparts. Bots don't require sleep either; therefore, they can work 24 hours a day, seven days a week if necessary. Bots will require supervision by humans to quality control (QC) the work being performed by the robots on behalf of the organization. The term *quality control* is a procedure or set of procedures intended to ensure that a performed service adheres to a defined set of quality criteria or that meets the requirements of the customer. Bots will also require human tweaks or recalibrations from time to time as the organization's needs change. They will become more and more prevalent in the future workforce, along with the use of artificial intelligence.

Artificial intelligence or AI for short will also emerge and impact the future of jobs. For example, in public education, artificial intelligence will enable schools to individualize the educational experience of every child who walks through their doors. I know because the organization I currently lead is doing just this. By using adaptive technologies and predictive algorithms, we can personalize the educational experience of each student to meet them where they are in terms of skill level and academic ability. The data we mine is used to inform decision-making and to customize a plan of action.

In the health care sector, AI is currently helping doctors during surgery and monitoring patients in recovery. A recent study published in *Nature* on the impact AI is having in the medical field stated that Google's artificial intelligence system could identify breast cancer more accurately than radiologists.[1] Virtual identification is an example of the potential that technology plays in having a positive impact on the lives of millions of people in the future. AI is being considered as a second reader with breast cancer patients to reduce the number of false positives and negatives. According to the CDC, breast cancer remains the second leading cause of cancer-related deaths in women throughout the United States, claiming almost 40,000 lives each year. Approximately one in eight women in the United States will develop breast cancer in their lifetime. Can you imagine a world where we could use AI to identify cancer in its infancy stage and proactively treat patients to reduce the number of deaths each year to a fraction of what it is today?

In the transportation sector, AI is also impacting the automobile industry. Self-driving cars and trucks will be a common reality in the next decade. Can you imagine a world where no one drives anymore? In the consumer sector, AI is helping companies like Amazon to make predictive suggestions about future purchases based on a customer's previous purchase history. Consumers can now verbally order groceries and goods without lifting a finger and have them delivered to their front door in two days or less. Artificial intelligence will work in combination with the natural selection of humans to create a more personal experience. Just as important as the technology itself are the future generations that will be working in collaboration with artificial intelligence.

---

1. Sara Reardon, "Rise of Robot Radiologists," *Nature* magazine (December 18, 2019), https://www.nature.com/articles/d41586-019-03847-z.

Generation Z are individuals who were born from approximately 1996 until 2010. This generation is also referred to as digital natives because they have never known life without the internet or digital devices. I have two sons, Bo and Jake, who were born into this generation, so I am fluent in what motivates Generation Z and what does not. This generation tends to value both money and security because they were children around the time of the great recession of 2008. Most Gen Zers prefer to work alone and can struggle at times to collaborate with others to complete projects on time. They are outstanding multitaskers and can seamlessly move from their laptop to phone to tablet to complete their work.

The next generation to hit the workforce will be Generation A (Alpha). This generation takes into account every individual born between 2011 and 2025. Our daughter, Bryn, was born in December 2010, but I consider her to be part of Generation A. There are some distinct differences between Bryn and her brothers. Bryn has spent the biggest part of her formative years completely immersed in technology. She started her own YouTube channel at the age of six. She records, edits, and uploads her vlogs, which typically center on the topic of gaming, to the internet using a green screen. By the age of eight, Bryn created multiple social media handles that we monitor. By the age of nine, she wanted to become an entrepreneur and start selling her own merchandise, which she created online. Today, she has amassed over one thousand followers on a popular social media app and done all of that before the age of 10. Are you and your organization ready for Generation A to enter the workforce? They will begin entering the labor pool around 2030.

Technology has become omnipresent in the twenty-first century. Moore's Law states that technology will keep doubling in power as prices keep halving. Technology, once out of reach for the less fortunate, has quickly become more affordable, allowing for access to become more mainstream and widespread even in the poorest of areas. Across the board, adoption will create the fourth Industrial Revolution in our country's history.

American history textbooks taught us that the first Industrial Revolution mechanized production of goods and services through the use of steam and water. The second Industrial Revolution allowed for mass production through the use of electricity. The third Industrial Revolution brought us digital and technological enhancements in the way we live and communicate with one another. The fourth Industrial Revolution is the global adoption of technology to improve the quality of life for all people.

The acceleration of innovation leaves in its wake a responsibility to shape the evolution of technology in a positive way for all humankind. The fourth Industrial Revolution has both enumerable potential and pitfalls as consequences to the choices we make. One of my favorite quotes about choices comes from legendary UCLA basketball coach John Wooden: "There is a choice you have to make in everything you do. So keep in mind that in the end, the choice you make, makes you."[2] Society must share a collective consciousness that seeks to serve rather than be served, that is built on empathy not ego, and that fosters ideas over immorality.

---

2. John Wooden, quoted in John Maxwell, *The Leadership Handbook: 26 Critical Lessons Every Leader Needs* (Nashville, TN: HarperCollins Leadership, 2015), 185.

Conclusion

The door to success that was locked when we began our journey together was simply a metaphor to your mind. The key to unlock the door to success comes down to your ability to control your thoughts. Your thoughts generate feelings, and your feelings determine your actions. Therefore, your future success will come down to your ability to discipline the thoughts that enter your mind.

The dawn of a new decade is upon us. Organizations that have taken a proactive approach by investing in their business and their employees will reap a bountiful harvest based on the new world order. By making the mental shift to evolve and embrace the tools and technologies of the twenty-first century, these organizations will prosper and lead their respective communities, states, and countries into a new era. Times have changed, and they will never be the same again.

The remote work environment is going to become more commonplace in all sectors of society. The benefits of creating a remote workforce are numerous. From company savings to productivity and even employee morale, the workforce of the future will be a blend of traditional and virtual work environments. The rise of this remote or virtual work environment will create a demand for leaders who are fluent in both worlds. Those leaders who choose to prepare for this eventuality will see a significant return on that investment. As we come to the end of our journey together and say goodbye, I hope you have found value in the nuggets of knowledge embedded within this book. I can assure you these leadership principles are timeless and will sustain you well into the future.

I welcome your stories of success applying these principles in your life. If you found value in this book, please consider sharing it with a family member, friend, or colleague. Knowledge is power, and I want to empower you to take control of your life and, ultimately, your future. I will leave you with two final thoughts: *I believe in you. Pay it forward.*

CPSIA information can be obtained
at www.ICGtesting.com
Printed in the USA
LVHW051358110222
710784LV00011B/1700